W9-CID-293

DISCARD

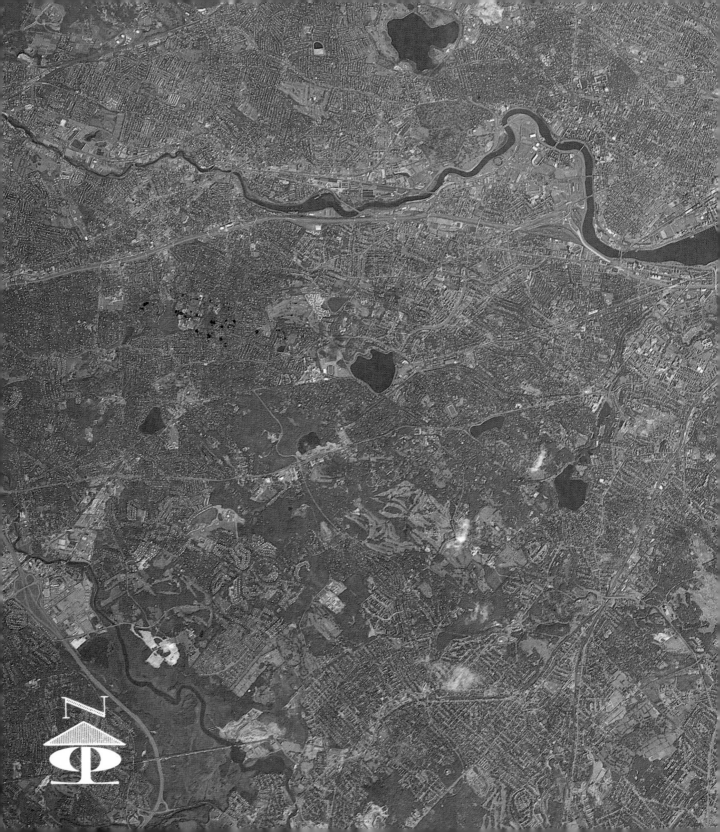

The New
Enchantment of America
MASSACHUSETTS

By Allan Carpenter

CHILDRENS PRESS, CHICAGO

ACKNOWLEDGMENTS

For assistance in the preparation of the revised edition, the author thanks:
JAMES J. KEENEY, Division of Tourism, Department of Commerce and Development, State of Massachusetts

American Airlines—Anne Vitaliano, Director of Public Relations; *Capitol Historical Society*, Washington, D. C.; *Newberry Library,* Chicago, Dr. Lawrence Towner, Director; *Northwestern University Library*, Evanston, Illinois; *United Airlines*—John P. Grember, Manager of Special Promotions; Joseph P. Hopkins, Manager, News Bureau.

UNITED STATES GOVERNMENT AGENCIES: *Department of Agriculture*—Robert Hailstock, Jr., Photography Division, Office of Communication; Donald C. Schuhart, Information Division, Soil Conservation Service. *Army*—Doran Topolosky, Public Affairs Office, Chief of Engineers, Corps of Engineers. *Department of Interior*—Louis Churchville, Director of Communications; EROS Space Program—Phillis Wiepking, Community Affairs; Charles Withington, Geologist; Mrs. Ruth Herbert, Information Specialist; Bureau of Reclamation; National Park Service—Fred Bell and the individual sites; Fish and Wildlife Service—Bob Hines, Public Affairs Office. *Library of Congress*—Dr. Alan Fern, Director of the Department of Research; Sara Wallace, Director of Publications; Dr. Walter W. Ristow, Chief, Geography and Map Division; Herbert Sandborn, Exhibits Officer. *National Archives*—Dr. James B. Rhoads, Archivist of the United States; Albert Meisel, Assistant Archivist for Educational Programs; David Eggenberger, Publications Director; Bill Leary, Still Picture Reference; James Moore, Audio-Visual Archives. *United States Postal Service*—Herb Harris, Stamps Division.

For assistance in the preparation of the first edition, the author thanks:
Consultants William P. Tsaffaras, Director, Bureau of Research and Statistics; William J. Sugrue, Director, Bureau of Commercial and Industrial Development; and State Department of Commerce and Development.

Illustrations on the preceding pages:

Cover photograph: Williamston, American Airlines, Inc.

Page 1: Commemorative stamps of historic interest
Pages 2-3: Pilgrim Village, Plymouth Plantation, American Airlines
Page 3: (Map) USDI Geological Survey
Pages 4-5: Boston area, EROS Space Photo, USDI Geological Survey, EROS Data Center

Project Editor, Revised Edition:
Joan Downing
Assistant Editor, Revised Edition:
Mary Reidy

Library of Congress Cataloging in Publication Data

Carpenter, John Allan, 1917-
Massachusetts.

(His The new enchantment of America)
SUMMARY: A history of the state and a description of its sites of interest and its natural and human treasures.
1. Massachusetts—Juvenile literature.
[1. Massachusetts]. I. Title. II. Series: Carpenter, John Allan, 1917- The new enchantment of America.
F64.C3 1978 974.4 78-3785
ISBN 0-516-04121-5

Contents

The Minuteman statue.

A True Story to Set the Scene

MAN OF THE HOUR

Plans for that day at Concord in 1875 had been made several years before, but the real beginning occurred just a hundred years earlier, in 1775, when the British marched out of Boston, cut down American volunteers at Lexington, and hurried on to Concord. At almost every farm the men had snatched their rifles from the racks above their fireplaces and hurried off to meet the enemy. The trained British troops were turned back after trying to cross the "rude bridge."

Concord was making plans for a gala celebration for the hundredth anniversary of that epic moment in history. In his will, Ebenezer Hubbard had left a thousand dollars for a memorial to those farmers who became soldiers in a minute, and went into history as the Minutemen.

Finding a sculptor to create a memorial was not easy. There were few good ones in America. A local man, only twenty-one years old, had some training in sculpture. He was Daniel Chester French, son of prominent Judge Henry Flagg French of Concord. When Dan French heard about the memorial, he began making drawings and clay models, and finally took one of the models to the committee headed by Mr. Ralph Waldo Emerson.

The committee had confidence in young Dan French's ability. They had all known him and had given him encouragement in the past. However, they would pay only his expenses, and he would have to contribute his services. "I have never made a statue," Dan French wrote to his brother. "I wonder whether I can do it. This time next year I shall *know!*"

The first unclothed model of the Minuteman statue was made, and the young artist needed examples of clothing worn at the time of the Revolution. From his neighbors' attics all over town came carefully and lovingly preserved parts of the Minuteman costume—homespun breeches with shilling buttons at the knee, powder horn, musket, even an antique plow, found after much searching.

As the 3-foot (.91 meters) model progressed, the proud people of

9

Concord kept coming to the artist's small room to view the results. This procession included some great names—Alcott, Longfellow, Emerson, and others. Finally the first model was ready for plaster casting. Dan French had never cast a model. He got a large amount of plaster, and he and his whole family pitched in, with much advice and assistance from the Judge. At one point the mold broke and disaster threatened, but at last everything turned out well, crowning the young artist's intense three months of work.

Then French was ready to make the life-size model in clay from which a bronze casting could be made. He took a studio in Boston. When he could not find a model, he borrowed a plaster copy of the *Apollo Belvedere* from the Boston Athenaeum. This ancient Roman figure made a strange sight in the studio, wearing the jaunty hat, and partly draped with some of the clothes of a Minuteman. The distinguished people of the Boston area often dropped in to praise or criticize. At last, the statue was finished. The United States Congress appropriated enough brass cannon and money to have the statue cast professionally.

On the day of dedication, the weather was cold. Judge French wrote his son that he was afraid more people would die that day of the cold than died in the battle they came to celebrate. President Grant, his Cabinet, other Washington celebrities, and the great of Massachusetts were all there along with a United States military band. There were notable speeches. Mr. Emerson read his poem, the first stanza of which had been cut into the base of the statue:

"By the rude bridge that arched the flood,
    Their flag to April's breeze unfurled,
Here once the embattled farmers stood,
    And fired the shot heard round the world."

The great man made a dramatic sweep of his arm, and the statue this crowd of thousands had come to see, stood before them. The day had been dark, but just at that moment a shaft of sunlight broke through the clouds, lighting the statue as if with a spotlight. President U.S. Grant and his Cabinet rose to their feet; there was great applause. This was one of the moments of tribute to the greatness of Massachusetts' people and of her heritage.

The bridge at Concord the British soldiers tried to cross.

Later that day the crowd of 5,000 held a banquet to celebrate. His first work had made the young artist famous almost overnight, but Daniel French was not present; he was away in Italy studying.

His later work included the wonderful shining, gold *Statue of the Republic,* one of the hits of the 1893 World's Fair in Chicago, still admired by Chicagoans today. Daniel Chester French went on to create what is possibly the most awe-inspiring and most looked-at work of art in the world—his enormous, magnificent, seated marble statue of Abraham Lincoln in the Lincoln Memorial at Washington.

11

Scituate Harbor, a small boating harbor near Boston in Cape Cod Bay, provides safe anchorage for hundreds of pleasure craft.

Lay of the Land

A ROCKY PILGRIM

A small boulder, protected by a marble canopy at the town of Plymouth, is the famous Plymouth Rock. The history, legends, and doubts that have grown up about this rock are generally well known, but possibly only a few people realize that this famous landmark of the Pilgrims was itself a kind of pilgrim, a transplanted "stranger" in a foreign land.

No one knows where it came from. Over the years it was pushed, shoved, rolled, dragged—forced inch by inch across the land in the grip of an icy hand—until it finally came to rest. Here it waited over the centuries to take its place in the American story.

Bringing of the Plymouth Rock was an insignificant part of the labor of the great glaciers—those mighty sheets of ice that formed far to the north and pushed their way across the country carrying everything in their path before them. In contrast to Plymouth Rock is mighty House Rock near Weymouth, which got its name from being as big as a house. It is thought to be the largest rock left in Massachusetts by the glaciers. Over a period of millions of years, these glaciers came and went, covering the land with a sheet of ice sometimes several thousand feet thick. The last one probably melted about 11,000 years ago.

When the ice disappeared, the face of the land had been altered dramatically. Stony upland pastures, river terraces, streamlined hills, and hollows that filled with water to make lakes—all were created by the glaciers. A very large lake was left in the Connecticut River Valley and may have remained there as long as 40,000 years until it drained.

The most dramatic of all, however, was the great mound of earth, called a terminal moraine, left by the glaciers. This mound of sand, gravel, and rock was pushed out into the sea for 70 miles (about 113 kilometers) to form the odd-shaped peninsula that we call Cape Cod.

The two principal islands of Massachusetts—Nantucket and Martha's Vineyard—were also formed by the glaciers.

Cape Cod forms the most striking single geographic feature of Massachusetts. This part of Massachusetts that extends eastward has been compared in shape to a fishhook or to a man's arm with a fist upraised. It has a shoreline of 300 miles (about 483 kilometers), and no part of Cape Cod is more than 6 miles (about 10 kilometers) from saltwater. It faces four bodies of water—the Atlantic, Cape Cod Bay, Buzzards Bay, and Nantucket Sound.

The coastline of Massachusetts is highly irregular, the result of centuries of interaction of sea and wind on glacial debris and rock.

Massachusetts lies within two major physical provinces: the Coastal Plain province and the New England province of the Appalachian highlands. Included in the highlands are the Taconic Range, with Mount Greylock, Massachusetts' highest peak, and the southern end of the Green Mountains. These latter are worn-down roots of an old range that once was higher and more rugged. The Berkshire Hills are mostly the result of ancient erosion.

CHARGOGGAGOGGMANCHUAGGAGOGGCHAUBUN-AGUNGAMAUGG AND OTHER WATERS

One of the largest lakes in Massachusetts is far from being the largest anywhere else, but it certainly can claim to have the biggest name. The title of this lake in its original Indian language simply means "You fish on your side. I fish on my side; nobody fish in the middle." The Indians would say: "Chargoggagoggmanchuaggagogg-chaubunagungamaugg." In Massachusetts there are nearly 3,000 great ponds or lakes. One of the smallest bodies of water, Walden Pond, has a worldwide reputation because of the writing of the most famous dweller on its shores—Henry David Thoreau. There are 365 lakes and ponds on Cape Cod alone.

There are 4,320 miles (about 6,952 kilometers) of streams in Massachusetts, forming 19 river systems. The most important of these rivers is the Connecticut River. Massachusetts rivers on the list of principal rivers of the United States compiled by the Geological Survey include the Merrimac and the Housatonic. Other important rivers are the Charles, Blackstone, Nashua, Concord, Mystic, Taunton, and Ipswich. The river pattern of Massachusetts is rather unusual. The Hoosic River drains north and then west. The Housatonic rises in the same swampy area, but flows southward. Several streams flow swiftly from the western mountains and have a tendency to flash flood.

The majestic Connecticut River has almost tied itself in knots in some places to form sweeping curves called oxbows. One of these, simply called The Oxbow, has been completely cut off from the river itself and now forms a separate lake.

MISCELLANEOUS FEATURES—INCLUDING THE WEATHER

An outstanding natural feature of Massachusetts is the beautiful natural bridge near North Adams. It was carved out of the white marble by wind and water over the centuries. In that area the same forces have also cut a breathtaking gorge through the white marble. Nathaniel Hawthorne described the beauties of this area in his *American Notebook*.

Other rugged features of Massachusetts are the Jambs, a gorge formed by a brook near Savoy, and Purgatory Chasm near Sutton, a half-mile-long (about .8 kilometers) fissure carved through rock.

In locations where the surface is exposed have been found the records of 600 million years of geology. Even volcanic rocks may be found in some areas. Dinosaur remains from 200 million years ago are those of smaller animals from 3 to 9 feet (.91 to 2.74 meters) in length, but larger tracks have been found. Fossil plants indicate that at one time the climate must have been much milder.

Today the winters are long but not too severe. The autumn weather is superb, enhanced by the vivid colors of the fall foliage. Because it stretches its arm so far into the Atlantic, Cape Cod has a milder climate with more sunshine, as does Nantucket Island. This is due mainly to the warm Atlantic Gulf Stream. The meeting of the warm Gulf Stream and the cold Labrador Current is an unusual one in oceanography.

15

Footsteps on the Land

THEY MET THE BOAT

Less is known about the earliest inhabitants of Massachusetts than of some of the other states. Our only knowledge of early peoples comes from the materials they left behind, and not many relics have been found. Some modest stone implements have been found, but no prehistoric tobacco pipes, axes, pottery, or imposing mounds of earth from a very early period.

At some unknown time, Algonquin Indians from the west began to migrate to present-day Massachusetts, and eventually they killed or mingled with the earlier inhabitants. Invasion by the fierce Iroquois upset and altered this Algonquin culture, so that the first Europeans found a mixture of Algonquin and Iroquois customs.

Seven principal groups occupied the area during the period of early European contact with the region. They were the Mohican, Nauset, Nipmuc, Pennacook (with their seven bands), Pocomtuc, Wampanoag, and Massachuset, who gave their name to the commonwealth. The Massachuset lived in the Great Blue Hill region south of present-day Boston, and the name Massachuset is supposed to mean "near the great hill or mountain."

All of the Indians lived by hunting, fishing, and farming. They raised squash, corn, beans, pumpkins, and even artichokes in their gardens, as well as the tobacco that meant so much to them. They were familiar with fertilization of the soil, using fish for this purpose. They hunted with bow and arrow and went on the warpath armed with club and tomahawk. Some carried wooden shields for defense. They made earthen pipes and clay cooking pots, and other simple handwork.

The Algonquin of Massachusetts were conscious of class distinctions. The principal chiefs inherited their titles and were often assisted by lesser chiefs and others of royal blood. The shaman, or

Opposite: Fall foliage in Pioneer Valley.

medicine man, held great power. Divorce was easy and common, and women could obtain a divorce as easily as men.

FIRST SAILS ON THE HORIZON

For a very long time the Indians had known of the Europeans who came from across the seas in their big canoes pulled by white clouds.

Some say the region was first visited by Europeans almost 500 years before Columbus made his voyage. Did Leif, son of the Norse leader Eric the Red, visit present-day Massachusetts in the year 1004? Had other adventurous European voyagers also touched those shores before 1492? Many arguments are heard on both sides, and it is still a mystery. Remains of a house of unknown origin, now called the Norse Wall House, have been unearthed in Provincetown. Its foundation stones were of a type not found on Cape Cod, but they could have been carried by the Norsemen as ballast in their ships. Others say that possibly the Norsemen sailed up the Bass River to Pollins Pond and that they also may have discovered Martha's Vineyard. Discoveries made since 1960 largely discredit the latter.

The first European actually known to have touched the soil of present-day Massachusetts was John Cabot in his voyage of 1497-98. This voyage gave England the basis for her claim to the region.

In 1578 Queen Elizabeth gave Sir Humphrey Gilbert a patent for colonization of southern New England, but he died in a storm at sea before he could accomplish this. At this time it was estimated that at least four hundred ships were regularly whaling and fishing off Massachusetts' shores, especially crews from Spain and France. Most of these ships carried on trade with the Indians, so that the native population had considerable contact with Europeans before 1600.

In 1602 Captain Bartholomew Gosnold caught such large quantities of codfish in the region of a great peninsula that he named it Cape Cod, a name it has kept ever since. Captain Gosnold also did some exploring of the area and is credited with discovering an island which he named Martha's Vineyard in honor of his daughter. In the same year, this energetic Englishman built a temporary fort at present-day Buzzards Bay and later sailed back to England with a remarkable cargo from the New World. It is strange to think that what may have been the first export shipment from New England's land was a cargo of sassafras.

The French colonizer, Samuel de Champlain, visited Stage Harbor in 1606, and Captain John Smith is supposed to have visited Massachusetts in 1614. His enthusiastic description of the land resulted in the establishment of small colonies for fishing and trading, but these were not permanent.

THE PILGRIMS

A group of dissenters from the established Church of England, called Separatists, sailed to Holland to make new homes, but they became unhappy there. At last they decided to seek homes in the New World. They were equipped for the journey by a group of London financiers and set out in the *Mayflower* on the long voyage.

They intended to settle on the James River in Virginia, but were thrown off their course, and landed November 11, 1620, on the bleak shores of Cape Cod Bay where Provincetown is today, becoming, indeed, Pilgrims in a new land. They remained there for five weeks until they felt that they could not support themselves in that region and would have to find a more suitable spot. The desperately hungry Pilgrims borrowed corn from the Indians on present-day Corn Hill in order to sustain themselves.

While they lived on the ship at anchor off Provincetown, the Pilgrims succeeded in producing a government for themselves that was to be a model not only for all future colonies but in the establishment of all succeeding governments of free men. This was the Mayflower Compact.

It may be wondered why the Pilgrims sailed on in the winter weather. But they left Provincetown, and on December 21 this little band of 102 religious refugees—men, women, and children—reached the land they decided to call home and which they named Plymouth in honor of the city in England.

Whether or not that first party headed their landing boat toward a large boulder on the shore and stepped onto the natural dock it provided is open to question. In any event, that Plymouth Rock has become a symbol of the momentous event.

Most of the Pilgrims stayed on the ship for about a month until a common house could be made for shelter. They began this work on the day after Christmas, 1620.

Some of the earliest houses were English wigwams, cone-shaped huts built on slanting poles, covered with reeds or brush and finished with clay or turf.

No one in our modern age of comfort, convenience, and luxury can imagine the hardships of that first winter, when many of the necessities of life were lacking. Those who died of want or disease were buried secretly on peaceful Cole's Hill overlooking the harbor. Corn was planted over their graves to keep the Indians from knowing how weak the colony was becoming. By March almost half of the group had died. In spite of difficulties, they assembled in the first common house and on February 27, 1621, held the first popular election on American soil.

Before long, the Pilgrims built the kind of saw pits they were familiar with in England and turned out lumber for building frame houses. In the spring, they planted their crops. Within a year they were able to load the ship *Fortune* with furs, lumber, and produce. To their great misfortune, this valuable cargo was captured by the French as a prize, and most of the efforts of that first awful year were lost. Nevertheless, as early as 1623, Governor William Bradford was able to write about the construction of "great houses in pleasant situations," which seems almost miraculous after such a desperate beginning. Leyden Street was already an avenue of pleasant homes.

However, without the kindness and help of the Indians, the Pilgrim settlement might have been impossible. They settled on lands of Massasoit, Wampanoag chieftain, and in April of 1621 the Pilgrims and Massasoit entered into an oral treaty on Strawberry Hill—one of the first treaties between Indians and Europeans. The terms of this treaty were faithfully kept by Massasoit throughout his lifetime, for fifty-four years.

Plymouth Rock, the symbol of the Pilgrims' landing.

Other unusual and helpful Indians in the earliest days of settlement were Samoset and Squanto. In March of 1621, just two months after they first landed at Plymouth, the Pilgrims were startled by an Indian who called out in English "Welcome, Englishmen." This was Samoset. He had learned English in Maine from fishermen.

Squanto made many claims. It is said that he had been taken to London in 1605 in the party of Captain George Weymouth, came back to Cape Cod with Captain John Smith in 1614, returned to England in the same year and then made his way back to America in 1619. He proved extremely useful as an interpreter and in many other ways.

TO ASK THE LORD'S BLESSING

After all their hardships of the first year, the Pilgrims were determined to have a real holiday before the winter of 1621 set in. They invited their Indian friends to join with them in celebration of the harvest festival and to praise the Lord for their new bounty of crops, game, and wild fruits.

The tiny Pilgrim band of fifty-five was a little dismayed when Massasoit arrived with a group of ninety Indians, instead of the few braves they expected, but the Indians had brought five deer to help the party. There were only five Pilgrim women and a few girls to cook for a group of 145.

21

Geese, turkey, and venison roasted on spits. Venison stew and clam chowder bubbled in great iron pots over the open fires. Oysters and lobsters steamed in the coals. Fish and eels were also on the menu. Dried fruits and berries were on hand, and there were plenty of wild cranberries around, but probably the Pilgrims could not spare the sugar to use them. They may have placed some of their dried fruits in folds of dough to make the ancestor of our modern pie. Corn biscuits and bread and Indian pudding (cornmeal combined with molasses boiled in a bag) were prepared. Squanto had taught the colonists how to make these last delicacies. There may even have been popcorn balls. Long before the colonists came, Indians had enjoyed popcorn made into balls with maple syrup.

While the women worked, the men had contests of strength and skill—marksmanship with bows and arrows, jumping, racing, and games. Miles Standish drilled his troops to the wonderment of the Indians. The eating and festivities continued for three days, giving the weary Pilgrims great relief from their difficult life of the past months.

LAND OF THE PILGRIMS' PRIDE

More settlers were coming over from England and some were striking out into other parts of the area. Weymouth (then called Wessagusset), founded in 1622, became the second settlement in Massachusetts. In 1624 Samuel Maverick, at the age of twenty-two, set up the first permanent home on Boston Harbor. Salem was founded in 1626. In that same year, the English settlers cooperated with the Dutch from New Amsterdam to set up a trading post at Aptuxcet, near present-day Bourne. This probably was the first post of its kind in America.

A Royal Charter was granted to the Massachusetts Bay Company in 1629, a document that formed the basis for democratic government in the Bay Colony. Governor John Winthrop set sail for Massachusetts Bay in 1630, with 800 Puritans who intended to set up a Puritan commonwealth, governed by Biblical principles. Like the

Pilgrims, they arrived too late to plant crops, and during the first year 200 of the Puritan settlers died, mostly of starvation.

The Puritans found the home of the first resident in present-day Boston—William Blackstone (or Blaxton). He was a graduate of Cambridge University in England, but could not stand civilization and became a recluse. He had bought the whole of Boston peninsula from the Indians. When the Puritans arrived he treated them well and sold them all but 6 acres (about 2.4 hectares) of his property, which was a more healthful region than Charlestown where they had first settled. And so with the cooperation of Blackstone, Winthrop, and the Puritans, Boston was founded in 1630. Within the first four years several thousand Englishmen came to Boston. By 1640, only ten years after its founding, 16,000 had arrived in Boston, coming for both religious and economic reasons. The Puritan settlement was immensely more important than the more publicized Pilgrim Colony of Plymouth, although Plymouth's contribution must never be underestimated.

These first ten years were ones of amazing progress for the Massachusetts Bay Colony. The first General Court was held in 1630. In 1634 the first Board of Selectmen in New England was elected. By 1635 Concord had become the foremost inland penetration of the wilderness. Also in that year, the General Court appropriated 400 pounds to establish a college—more than the whole annual tax income of the colony. This, of course, became Harvard. In 1638 the Ancient and Honorable Artillery Company was founded—the oldest military organization in America. Also in that year the annual Duxbury Fair was begun, the first in the United States.

Plymouth Rock is preserved in a classical structure built in 1920.

A PERIOD OF DISTURBANCE

In 1662 the long period of harmony with the Indians in Massachusetts ended with the arrest of the Indian leader, Wamsutta. It was becoming increasingly clear to Indian leaders such as King Philip, son of kindly Chief Massasoit, and brother of Wamsutta, that if white settlement continued, the Indians would soon be forced from their lands. He determined to drive the white settlers out and laid his plans very carefully. However, he was forced to begin the war before he was ready because his plans were discovered.

During King Philip's War great tragedy occurred on both sides. One out of every ten of the five thousand Englishmen of military age was killed. Thirteen towns were completely burned, six hundred homes ruined, and six hundred settlers killed. In the Bloody Brook massacre of 1675, Deerfield was burned and all settlers were killed or taken into slavery. At first the Indians met with great success, but eventually the superior power of the government turned the tide. Philip was killed by one of his own men, his wife and son sold into slavery, and the war came to an end. Tremendous numbers of Indians had been killed during the struggle.

At one time Roger Williams had lectured the rulers of Massachusetts in defense of the Indians: "Your patent from King James is but idle parchment. James has no more right to give away or sell Massasoit's lands and cut and carve his country than Massasoit has to sell King James' kingdom or to send Indians to colonize Warwickshire." However, in the case of the colonists the ancient doctrine of might makes right applied, and Indian influence in the area came almost to an end.

The Indian had not been entirely without friends in Massachusetts. John Eliot, Apostle to the Indians, helped to establish what were called Praying Towns, centers of learning where Indians were educated and taught Christianity. Amazingly, thirty of these Praying Towns were established. By 1663 Eliot had even managed to translate part of the Bible into the local Indian language, the first time this had been done. The first brick building erected at Harvard was built for Indian students, but not enough of them attended to make it worthwhile. However, at least one Indian, Caleb Cheeshahteamuck, graduated from Harvard as early as 1665.

Many Indians accepted Christianity. The Christian Indians wanted to take no part in King Philip's War, but they were suspected of disloyalty by both Europeans and Indians. Most of them were exiled to Long Island and Deer Island where they suffered terribly. The treatment of the Christian Indians of Massachusetts has been called one of the blacker pages of our history.

For thirty years the Massachusetts Bay Colony remained almost totally independent of England. From 1660 on, the Mother Country began to establish growing control, until in 1691 Massachusetts became a Royal Colony. Church membership was no longer a requirement for voting. Until this time, also, Plymouth had remained a separate and independent Pilgrim colony. This type of self-contained corporate colony was unlike any that had grown up in the south, in Virginia, North Carolina, New Jersey, and New York.

MASS HYSTERIA BEWITCHES

A slave girl named Tituba from the West Indies was responsible for touching off one of the waves of hysteria that now seems completely senseless.

Tituba liked to tell Voodoo stories of her native islands to the young girls of Salem. This proved too much for the girls' imagination; they screamed and claimed to see dreadful things in the dark. When a local doctor said they had been bewitched, the girls accused Tituba and two elderly women who were much disliked by the community. They were charged with being in league with the Devil and were quickly put to death.

This was only a part of several years of dread in Salem and other Massachusetts communities, during which almost anyone might be accused of witchcraft by someone who had a grudge against them or who wildly imagined some evil thing they had done. However, it must be said that the colony was no different in this than Europe, where the witchcraft scare also raged.

The Witch House in Salem.

At Danvers, when Rebecca Nurse was accused of witchcraft, her courageous neighbors came to her defense in spite of the danger to themselves, but the good woman was hanged. In a few cases those accused were saved. At Beverly, Mistress Hale, wife of the Puritan minister, was accused, but her life had been so saintly that the authorities were forced to let her go.

One accused witch, Mary Webster, was hanged in 1683 and then buried in the snow. In some way she managed to revive after the awful ordeal and lived for several years until she died a natural death. Even the wife of Governor Phips was accused of witchcraft, but with this the Governor sternly brought the awful period to a close. The bodies of nineteen condemned witches had dangled on Gallows Hill at Salem. Twenty had been put to death at Danvers. Amesbury was another center of witchcraft hysteria.

A TRIBUTE TO OUR STERN FOREFATHERS

The Europe the first Massachusetts settlers fled was one in which the people were forced to work and worship in the established ways. They had little hope of ever freeing themselves from depressing restrictions, and almost no prospect of raising their status in the world.

Settlers sought to establish a brotherhood of believers in which everyone had the same beliefs and each would have an equal voice in managing all the affairs of the community. These people were willing to risk the awful hardships of a voyage of many weeks on the Atlantic and the perils of a wilderness.

Early settlers had to work constantly just to stay alive. It is no wonder, then, that they distrusted slackers and those who had different beliefs. They had suffered every hardship to preserve a community in which these beliefs were held.

We must credit them with an unbelievably strong ideal—the right of each individual to control his own conscience and reach his own decisions. This ideal has become the basis for the American dream. They were the pioneers in the almost completely untried field of universal human rights.

Of course, they had human failings. They had many lapses from justice and mercy. When Thomas Morton set up his colony of Merrymount (now Quincy), he opposed Puritanism. Morton even encouraged such practices as the celebration of May Day. Miles (Myles) Standish was ordered to arrest him. For this and other excesses, Morton was sent back to England, and when he returned he was sent back again.

The same spirit of revolt that drove Puritans to the new land drove some of their members out to find new freedom in the wilderness. Roger Williams and his followers were persecuted by the Puritans for their beliefs. Along with Anne Hutchinson, who disputed the divine inspiration of ministers, they were able to establish centers for their beliefs in Rhode Island. Quaker Elizabeth Horton was lashed and left bleeding in the wilderness; other Quakers were persecuted and executed.

It was said that John Cotton and his descendants, Cotton Mather and Increase Mather, had hardened Puritanism into a state in which the clergymen became the rulers.

As in the case of William Pynchon, dissenters of all types were persecuted. Pynchon, founder of Springfield, was condemned for his book *The Meritorious Price of Our Redemption*. The book was burned, and he returned to England.

Nevertheless, the individual zealots who managed to defeat "freedom" gained only a temporary victory. From 1620 on, the congregations were never forced to give up their authority to remove their ministers. And this was frequently done upon a vote of the membership.

Even more important, the Pilgrims and Puritans evolved a democratic governmental method—the town meeting—and in this way made one of the greatest contributions to the nation's political development. Both Watertown and Plymouth claim to be the cradle of the town meeting form of government. In contrast to England, in the town meeting every church member, and later every freeman, had an equal voice. Plymouth governed itself almost from the start in this way. However, Watertown first developed the more formal methods when it elected New England's first Board of Selectmen in 1634. Under the Reverend George Phillips, the church at Watertown was as democratic as the town meeting. With his remarkable guidance and that of the other Watertown founders, John Oldham and Sir Richard Saltonstall, Watertown remained free of Quaker and witchcraft persecutions. This was also true in other places.

The merit of the Pilgrim and Puritan founders has been summed up by the historian A.L. Rowse who states: "They did exemplify higher standards than any other English society, and this more than any other was the making of the nation."

PRELUDE TO REVOLUTION

The fierce love of individual freedom and the democratic tradition of the first century of Massachusetts' life made the people unhappy with the King's growing control. This began a series of events that led directly to the Revolution.

By the early 1700s Massachusetts had found in the sea the natural resources Nature had denied it on the land—the wealth of fishing and the greater wealth of maritime trade. Even during the French and Indian War from 1756 to 1763, Massachusetts continued to carry on what was called the triangular trade. Rum was sent to Africa in exchange for slaves. These unfortunate people were taken to the French West Indies in exchange for molasses and sugar, which was taken back to Massachusetts to make more rum. Some of the great fortunes of Massachusetts were founded on this illicit and inhuman trade.

After the war with France, the British began to enact measures designed to pay for the war and to regulate American trade. The Sugar Act of 1764 almost abolished the foreign trade on which Massachusetts depended. In 1765 the Stamp Act required many of the goods in trade, legal documents, and newspapers to carry British revenue stamps, making the cost much higher. The people of Massachusetts were peculiarly sensitive to commercial regulation from England. As early as 1687 the Reverend John Wise from Ipswich had denounced taxation without representation. These acts would almost have wiped out the prosperity of the colony, because it depended so heavily on imports and exports.

Massachusetts led a boycott, along with rioting, that spread throughout the American colonies. Those protests were so successful that the Stamp Act was repealed, and the Sugar Act revised in 1766.

Still the Mother Country could not understand these troublesome colonial children. Government was expensive and they must be made to pay their share. In 1770 the Townshend Acts were passed, making the people pay a duty on glass, tea, paint, and other imports. More riots took place, and the Townshend Acts were also repealed.

This time, however, British troops were sent to Boston to try to keep order. On March 5, 1770, when a mob gathered outside the Old State House, the troops fired, and six citizens were killed. Three days later the bells of Boston, Roxbury, Charlestown, and

Destruction of Tea at Boston Harbor,
a painting by Currier & Ives.

Cambridge tolled in mourning as the victims were solemnly borne through the streets of Boston past the silent crowd to their burial site. This event has gone down in history as the Boston Massacre.

In 1773 still another revenue act was passed by Parliament in England. This Tea Act was the last straw to many, since it seemed to give special favor to the British East India Company. Fiery Samuel Adams worked tirelessly to arouse the people of Massachusetts against the tyranny of Britain. It was Adams who planned to have fifty men disguise themselves as Indians in the Old South Meeting House. From there they rushed to Griffin's Wharf, where the merchant ships lay, loaded with crates of tea from the East Indies. With whoops and shouts they swarmed on board and tossed tea worth 15,000 pounds into the harbor in a protest called the Boston Tea Party.

Because of this "tea party," the furious British closed the port of Boston and revoked the colony's charter. The other American colonies felt great sympathy for the people of Massachusetts. Supplies and assistance poured in to help Massachusetts' people meet their needs, now that the all-important port was closed.

The colonists grew bolder. In August, 1774, the people of Great Barrington seized the courthouse and prevented the King's Court from holding its session. A marker in front of the courthouse today recalls this as the first act of open armed resistance to British rule in America.

A call went out for delegates from every colony to meet in September to plan the best method of resisting the violations of their rights. Actual independence was still not being considered. Behind locked doors the Massachusetts Assembly selected delegates to this Continental Congress. Through the keyhole, Royal Governor Thomas Gage angrily shouted that the Assembly was dissolved and all further action was illegal, but no one paid the slightest attention.

Massachusetts had come to the end of one era and faced the beginning of a new day, one filled with both inconceivable perils and progress.

Right: The Midnight
Ride of Paul Revere,
by W.R. Leigh.
Below: The Battle of
Bunker Hill.

Yesterday and Today

LAND WHERE OUR FATHERS DIED

On the evening of April 18, 1775, one of the great dramas of world history began to unfold. General Thomas Gage, the British commander at Boston, sent seven hundred of his troops to capture a large supply of munitions the patriots had assembled at Concord. It was feared that he also planned to arrest the two men who had done most to bring about the rebellion of the colonists—Samuel Adams and John Hancock. Gage believed them to be at Lexington.

As the British troops began their overland march, the famous signal was given, and three loyal men—Dr. Samuel Prescott, Paul Revere, and William Dawes—flung themselves on their horses to alert the countryside. The headlong dash of Paul Revere was probably no more heroic or useful than that of the other two, and he was the only one of the three captured by the British, but Revere became immortal through the famous Longfellow poem "The Midnight Ride of Paul Revere."

The warning shouts of the three rang out as they galloped along, and everywhere patriots seized their guns and hurried off. At Lexington the British met thirty-eight armed patriots, heroic in military formation against such great odds. A marker near the spot bears the immortal instructions of American Captain John Parker: "Stand your ground. Don't fire unless fired upon. But if they mean to have war, let it begin here."

Eight Americans died when the British fired, but the Americans returned the volley, giving Lexington its claim as the birthplace of American independence.

After this "curtain raiser of the American Revolution," the British troops left the American troops to care for their wounded, and hurried on to Concord. The redcoats were able to destroy the American military supplies at Concord, but they were met by a troop of Minutemen on the famous Old North Bridge. "Here the embattled farmers stood and fired the shot heard round the world," giving Concord its share with Lexington as the Revolution's birthplace.

By this time angry Americans were streaming in from almost every cottage in the countryside.

The redcoats had to withdraw hurriedly and make their way back to Boston with colonial marksmen of deadly aim firing at them from behind every possible place of concealment. By the time the British arrived back in Boston, 247 had been killed, with colonial losses at only 88.

More and more American volunteers poured in to aid in the siege of Boston until eventually there were 20,000. General Artemus Ward was placed in command and given the task of outfitting and training this motley group, most without sufficient military training, experience, or supplies.

British General Gage decided he needed to strengthen his fortifications and on June 17 he moved to Breed's Hill. Here he met American troops who had fortified the hilltop only the day before. They are supposed to have been instructed, "Don't fire until you see the whites of their eyes." Somehow this battle has gone down in history bearing the name of nearby Bunker Hill instead of Breed's where it actually took place. The Americans withstood two fierce charges before their ammunition gave out and they were driven off in a third attack. It was neither a great defeat nor a victory for either.

On the day before the Battle of Bunker Hill took place, George Washington had accepted command of the Continental Army from the Continental Congress at Philadelphia. Most of that army, if it could be called an army, was engaged in bottling up the British at Boston, and Washington went to Boston to take active command. He suggested that the men wear hunting shirts until uniforms could be provided, and his genius for organization and training conceived many other measures to help knit the men into a more efficient fighting body in spite of the lack of most wartime essentials.

The siege of Boston continued until the spring of 1776. Meanwhile, over the snows of winter, dauntless Ethan Allen was sledding cannon captured at Fort Ticonderoga. When these were put in place on Dorchester Heights and Nooks Hill and began to lob their shots down on the British, the defenders knew they could not withstand the attack Washington must be about ready to launch. On March 17,

1776, British troops left Boston and sailed for Nova Scotia. With them went many Americans, called Tories, who remained loyal to Britain.

This was the first great American victory of the Revolution, and it gave the people great courage to continue the fight.

The commonwealth continued to do its share in the wartime effort. Even old men and women took an active part. A tablet at Arlington recalls an event that took place while the British were still in Massachusetts: "At this spot, April 19, 1775, the old men of Menotomy captured a convoy of eighteen men with supplies on the way to join the British at Lexington." Six of these British men escaped the old men and were fleeing down the road in panic when they met old Mother Batherick on the banks of Fresh Pond, digging dandelions. Exactly how the brave old lady was able to seize her rifle, take them off their guard, and capture six British grenadiers will never be known, but she marched them to prison in the town. These were not unusual examples of the fighting spirit and feats of bravery of the people of Massachusetts.

All over the commonwealth women were melting down their prized pewter to make bullets and meeting every sacrifice demanded by circumstances. Many brave women, such as Deborah Sampson of Plympton, dismayed that only men were allowed to fight, disguised themselves as men and went courageously into battle.

STATEHOOD AND AFTER

Many disastrous effects of the Revolution were evident in Massachusetts at the end of the war. Boston had declined from a city of 25,000 people to a mere 10,000. Much of the state's commerce had been ruined. The farmers were particularly hard hit, and the entire country felt the effects of an economic depression. Discontent grew to such an extent that a former soldier, Daniel Shays, led an uprising against the government. Shays' Rebellion hoped to stop the courts from imprisoning bankrupt farmers and to give the poor people other relief. They succeeded in closing the courts of Worcester. On February 27, 1787, about one hundred of them plundered Stockbridge and Great Barrington, but were routed at Ashley. They even threatened to take Boston but were overcome when they tried to capture the United States Arsenal at Springfield.

In the matter of government, the commonwealth at first joined with the other former colonies in the Articles of Confederation. When the new United States government was organized, Massachusetts became the sixth state in 1788.

The commonwealth's own constitution had been accepted eight years earlier. Massachusetts was the last of the original thirteen states to adopt a state constitution. However, this course of action proved to be wise because the original constitution of 1780 is still in use today, the oldest of all the states.

In the last ten years of the eighteenth century, Massachusetts entered a new period of prosperity based on what was called the China trade. Massachusetts' fast ships made the tremendously long voyage around Cape Horn carrying goods for trade. The wonderful sea otter, beaver, and other valuable furs of the Pacific Coast, from California to Alaska, could be purchased from the Indians for a few trinkets. It mattered little to the sea captains of Boston and Salem that such trade was generally forbidden by Spain, England, and Russia.

From the Pacific Coast of America, the dauntless skippers sailed their ships straight across the huge Pacific, stopping at Hawaii for more trade, then going on to China where the wealthy mandarins would pay tremendous prices for sea otter furs and other materials from America. On the return voyage the ships would be loaded with the rich goods of the Orient to be sold in America and Europe. Such a voyage might take three years to complete and might touch such exotic ports as Honolulu and Sitka, in Russian Alaska.

Later, Massachusetts' ships did a tremendous business with the Spanish of California in cow hides for Massachusetts' new shoe-making industries. Many of Massachusetts' people were at home all over the world and their thinking and conversation were in global terms.

A NEW CENTURY

When Thomas Jefferson was elected President, some Massachusetts women concealed their Bibles because they expected he would command them to be burned. During his second term, President Jefferson had problems with the British and French who interfered with American shipping. To overcome this he set up an embargo to cut off trade with Britain. This hurt Massachusetts' commerce very much. In fact, merchants were spelling the word embargo backwards as "O Grab Me," accusing the law of grabbing their wealth.

Later, the War of 1812, called "Mr. Madison's War," proved even more damaging to Massachusetts' shipping. In 1814 the General Court in Boston went so far as to issue a call for a convention to consider secession from the United States.

However, after the war a new day dawned for Massachusetts because of the manufacturing industries springing up everywhere.

Because of its religious beginnings, Massachusetts always had deep concern for human rights. A convention in 1820 made the state constitution more liberal. In 1833 church and state were separated. The first child labor law and the first minimum wage law for women and children were passed in 1836 and 1842. The commonwealth was the first in the country to create a State Board of Health, State Department of Insurance, and State Tuberculosis Sanitorium. A Women's Rights Convention was held at Worcester in 1850.

SPARKING THE DRIVE FOR FREEDOM

The inhuman institution of slavery caused even greater concern to some people of Massachusetts. Bond slavery had been forbidden in 1641. As early as 1791 the lower court at Worcester made a notable decision that the Declaration of Independence statement "all men are created equal" applied to blacks.

The more formal movement against slavery was begun in Boston in 1830 by William Lloyd Garrison. At that time such beliefs as his were considered traitorous, and a mob built a gallows in front of Garrison's home. At another time they took him from his office and would have lynched him if he had not been rescued by the mayor. In spite of opposition, Garrison founded his antislavery paper, *The Liberator,* in Boston in 1831.

In 1832 the New England Antislavery Society was formed in Boston, and in 1837 Wendell Phillips made his first antislavery speech in Faneuil Hall. The people responded slowly at first, but gradually large numbers joined the crusade against the ownership of one human being by another. Massachusetts led in the underground railroad movement in which various "stations" were set up to lead fugitive slaves from one safe point to another until they reached safety in Canada.

In Worcester mobs kept United States marshals from capturing runaway slaves, and the Free Soil party was formed there in 1848. This party led the way for the formation of the Republican party and the election of Abraham Lincoln. In fact, Massachusetts voted for the first presidential candidate of the Republican party, John C. Fremont, in 1856.

One of the most unusual antislavery organizations was the Massachusetts Emigrant Aid Company. This was formed to recruit abolitionists (those who opposed slavery) for emigration to Kansas. The slave owners of nearby Missouri were pouring into Kansas in such numbers that Kansas appeared to be well on its way to becoming another slave state. The Emigrant Aid Company worked with such devotion and enthusiasm at the job of funneling antislavery settlers into Kansas that the state was populated much more quickly than it might otherwise have been. Thanks to this work, the number of abolitionists in Kansas eventually passed that of the slave holders. After the most bitter period of disagreement over slavery before the Civil War, Kansas was admitted as a free state.

As the antislavery movement which began in Massachusetts spread throughout the North, the bitterness of those who opposed it increased in the South. Whether or not slavery could have been abolished without Civil War is a question that probably will remain unanswered, because the war came in 1861.

When President Lincoln called for volunteers, 1,500 Massachusetts men responded within four days. Colonel Robert Gould Shaw organized a regiment of black volunteers. When they courageously led the attack on Fort Wagner, Colonel Shaw and more than half of his brave men were killed.

As the war went on, the first draft in United States history proved necessary. This was tremendously unfair to poor people, because those with money could pay $300 and hire a substitute. In protest of this injustice, Boston suffered a draft riot in 1863, and the militia had to be sent to put down the disorders.

Notwithstanding the fact that there was opposition to some war measures, 160,000 Massachusetts men fought in the Civil War.

AFTER THE WAR

To celebrate the peace, Boston splurged with a Peace Jubilee. A special stadium seating 30,000 was built. The band included not 76 trombones but 84. There were 83 tubas and 83 trumpets, 75 drums and 330 strings, along with 119 woodwind instruments. A ten thousand voice chorus shouted the praises of peace, and a hundred firemen beat on anvils in the Anvil Chorus. It may not have been good, but it was loud. President Grant, who attended, was almost forced to hold his ears.

Much of the history of progress in Massachusetts after the Civil War relates to industry and transportation. One great milestone in transportation occurred in 1914. For more than two hundred years seafaring men had dreamed of a shortcut to eliminate the long and dangerous circumnavigation of Cape Cod. In that year the dream finally came true when the Cape Cod Canal was opened.

During World War I, 198,000 citizens of Massachusetts were in uniform. Of these 5,700 died.

MODERN MASSACHUSETTS

As the war ended, one of the most famous strikes in history took place when the policemen of Boston left their posts to protest the dismissal of eight policemen and also low wages, long hours, and poor working conditions. Beginning on September 9, 1919, Boston had no protection, and hoodlums swarmed in to take advantage of the situation. Seven people were killed in disorders that turned public opinion against the strikers. Governor Calvin Coolidge promptly called out the militia, and his forceful actions at that time did more to bring him to nationwide attention than anything else. By the tenth of November a new police force was on duty in Boston.

A year later, in 1920, further notoriety came to Boston with one of the most famous trials in American history. A shoe worker, Nicola Sacco, and a fish peddler, Bartolomeo Vanzetti, were accused of murder and payroll robbery. Because they had been anarchists who opposed any government, many felt that they were given unfair treatment at their trial. All over the world people protested the Sacco-Vanzetti death sentences. The Supreme Court of Massachusetts twice refused a new trial, and a committee of prominent citizens upheld the findings of the courts. Seven years after the trial, Sacco and Vanzetti were executed in the electric chair.

Because Massachusetts was so highly industrialized, the state was one of the first to feel the effects of the great worldwide depression beginning in the late 1920s. The problems caused by the depression were among the worst in any state. World War II brought the great manufacturing skills of Massachusetts again into full play. In that war 556,000 men and women of Massachusetts served in the armed forces and over 15,500 died.

A native of Springfield, Major-General Arthur MacArthur leads his
troops at the Battle of Callocan, as viewed from the Chinese
Church in the Philippines, during the Spanish-American War.
This was one of the campaigns that made him one of the state's major
modern military heroes, preceding his even more famous son, Douglas.

Mayflower II, *a touching reminder of the past.*

More than half of the twentieth century had passed when shipbuilders in Plymouth, England, began a job that took them back more than three hundred years. Using the exact building methods of olden days, they created as nearly as possible a replica of the *Mayflower*. With great ceremony the historic replica was launched and set its sails for America.

On June 12, 1957, the people of Provincetown sighted the sails of *Mayflower II* coming into view over the horizon, as the Indians may have done some 330 years before. Finally, *Mayflower II* was proudly anchored at Plymouth, within sight of Plymouth Rock, where it became one of the country's great tourist attractions.

Not since the time of the Adamses had Massachusetts placed a native son in the presidency. Consequently, it was a proud day for the commonwealth, especially for its many people of Irish descent, when in January 1961 John Fitzgerald Kennedy, born in Brookline, became the thirty-fifth President of the United States.

The saddest day for many came almost three years later when that same favorite son was assassinated in Dallas, Texas, on November 22, 1963.

To prepare for the new decade of the '70s, the state government was reorganized in 1971. One of the most difficult problems of the decade has been the dispute over forced busing in the Boston public schools to provide racial integration.

42

THE PEOPLE OF MASSACHUSETTS

For many years after the first settlements, almost everyone in Massachusetts was of English stock. But by 1930, over 65 percent of the state's population had a background other than English. Massachusetts had acquired more ethnic strains than any other state except New York. Into the Puritan commonwealth, enriching it with their varied Old World cultures, had come new Americans from many countries of Europe. Finns, Greeks, Lithuanians, and Turks have joined the Irish and Scots who arrived in numbers before the Civil War; French, Italians, Poles, Portuguese, Germans, and many more have cast their fortunes along with the descendants of those first immigrants, the Pilgrims and the Puritans. Today there are more people from Canada in Massachusetts than from any other country.

The firm and often harsh way of life laid down by the forefathers has remained in some ways almost to the present day. Not until 1929, for example, was a professional baseball game permitted in Boston on Sunday. John Hancock was once fined for taking a buggy ride on Sunday, and in the very early days plays were not allowed at all. Dramatic productions were advertised as moral lectures, and Shakespeare's *Macbeth* was given a new title, *A Dialogue on the Horrid Crime of Murder.* Even today Boston is still known as the place where many books are banned, following the example set by the New England Watch and Ward Society.

Modern Massachusetts is changing at a dizzy pace. The commonwealth is tenth in population and third in population density. The eastern seaboard is becoming one gigantic metropolitan community. City population, statewide, is now five to one over rural. The town meeting is now no longer adequate to the needs, and regional planning is taking its place.

What the future will bring no one can know. However, it is certain that the past has provided Massachusetts with a firm and magnificent foundation on which to build.

The commercial fishing port in Provincetown where fishing is the principal year-round industry. Provincetown depended on whaling and fishing for two hundred years, but in the beginning of the twentieth century it began to develop into a summer resort.

Natural Treasures

SWIMMING, FLYING, CRAWLING, BLOOMING THINGS

In the State House at Boston, opposite the Speaker's chair, suspended from the ceiling, dangles a carved, wooden fish. With the exception of Jonah's whale, this is probably the best-known water creature in the world—called the sacred cod of Massachusetts. In 1784, John Rowe moved the House that permission might be given to hang up the representation of a "Codfish." The pine carving has been hanging in the State House ever since as a symbol of the importance of the fishing industry to Massachusetts.

Today, sports fishing is tremendously popular. Saltwater sportsmen catch winter flounder, mackerel, striped bass, and, of course, cod. Popular freshwater fish include bass, pickerel, and trout. The trout of Cape Cod are particularly enjoyed. The shell fish of the area are prized both by lovers of good dining and collectors of shells. The shoreline of Cape Cod is especially rewarding to those interested in beach life.

Knobbed and channeled conch, surf and quahog clam, ribbed mussel shells, fiddler, horseshoe and blue crab, and starfish attract ardent beachcombers. Offshore are the spotted harbor seal, the rollicking dolphin, and occasionally, a finback whale.

Shore birds include the scurrying sandpiper, stately great blue heron, American egret, sanderling, ruddy turnstone, plover, and many others. Among the water birds, the best known are waddling gulls, white-winged scoters, cormorants, and loons. Thousands of eider ducks winter off Monomoy. In spring and fall great flocks of migrant birds are so dense they show up on radar screens like enemy aircraft.

Among land birds are the prized belted kingfisher, myrtle warbler, bob-white, red-eyed towhee, brown thrasher, sparrow hawk, yellow-shafted flicker, and whip-poor-will. Ruffed grouse are popular game birds, and wild turkey and pheasants have been introduced successfully.

"The great southward migration of monarch butterflies along the dunes of Cape Cod in September and October is the butterfly event of the year," according to Professor Alexander Klots. So many sometimes cluster on branches that they make "butterfly trees." The tiny bog copper butterfly is found only in cranberry bogs.

Deer, snowshoe hare, red fox, woodchuck, muskrat, and even the rare otter are found in Massachusetts. Woodside cottagers love to tempt the sprightly eastern chipmunk with peanuts. Public hunting grounds in Massachusetts cover 23,000 acres (about 9,308 hectares).

Wildflowers grow profusely. On Bartholomew's Cobbe (a rocky hill) alone are found 700 species of wildflowers and 220 kinds of birds. Even the seaweeds of shore areas—Irish moss, sea lettuce and poppers, kelp, rockweeks, maiden's hair—find their way into seaweed albums. Marsh grass, sedges, and rush are plucked for many rustic flower arrangements.

Massachusetts' state flower, trailing arbutus, thrives in its native soil. The moors of Nantucket Island are blanketed with purple heather. Bayberry, beach plum, seaside lavender, butter-and-eggs, aster, marsh sapphire, and even the rare and elusive stemless ladies slipper reward the lover of wild beauty.

In spite of its small size and large population, Massachusetts still has an abundance of natural wealth to be enjoyed. The people of Massachusetts have a long history of preserving and promoting their natural heritage. The Fish and Game Commission was established in 1865. Three national wildlife refuges in the commonwealth help to preserve the natural wealth for all people. The Cape Cod National Seashore is the second such area in the United States.

Visitors can learn about Massachusetts in such fine displays as that of the Blue Hills Trailside Museum 10 miles (about 16 kilometers) south of downtown Boston.

The state flower, the mayflower or trailing arbutus.

The state bird, the chickadee.

FORESTS AND MINERALS

Those not familiar with Massachusetts are frequently surprised at the extent of its beautiful forests. The scarlet maples; the butter-yellow birches fluttering over gleaming white bark; lacy, yellowing larches; the russets and maroons of oaks stand in sharp contrast against the deep, gleaming, green backdrop of hemlock and pine. Such scenes are often mirrored in placid azure ponds or calm streams and combine to make New England autumns true wonders. Every forested valley and mountainside becomes an unbelievable fairyland.

Commercial forests cover over 3,000,000 acres (about 1,200,000 hectares) of Massachusetts. Of these, most are in private hands. The Arnold Arboretum at Boston offers students and nature lovers the largest collection of imported living trees and shrubs in the United States.

Building stone, lime, aggregates, and clays are still found in important quantities in Massachusetts. Copper, corundum, emery, and iron were important at one time. Other metal ore of Massachusetts include asbestos, barite, chromium, feldspar, lead, manganese, mica, nickel, pyrite, silver, spodumene, talc, and zinc. Most of these were from small sources, commercially useful only in the early days.

Today one of the most valuable resources in the world is fresh water. Fortunately, Massachusetts is one of the few regions of the world expecting to have an adequate water supply by the year 2000.

*The electrical and related industries of
Massachusetts employ more people than any other.*

People Use Their Treasures

The people of Massachusetts have been pioneers in most of the important activities through which man makes his living—in transportation from clipper ship through atom-powered vessels, in commerce with the Triangular trade and the China trade, in industry in a dozen different fields, and in fishing and whaling.

RESERVOIR OF INGENUITY

For 300 years Massachusetts has nurtured a climate of creativity. That is, conditions have been right for new industries and ideas to develop, and for imaginative people to invent new methods and devices.

The first ironworks in the United States was established in 1643 only twenty-three years after the Pilgrims landed. In that same year the first fulling mill for treating wool was built at Rowley. The country's first cotton mill sprang up at Beverly in 1788.

Massachusetts' greatest resource in the manufacturing industry was the skill of the average Yankee farmer. No stores were available in the wilderness to sell him what he needed. He had to make many of the necessities of life by his own ingenuity—from furniture to farm implements and kitchen utensils.

As agriculture developed in the West, and as new transportation opened up eastern markets for western goods, the Massachusetts farmer found his products could no longer compete, but he had the skills that the new factories needed. So Massachusetts began the change from farming to industrial production, a process which has continued ever since, and skills have remained at a very high level. After 1816, the growth of industry in Massachusetts was rapid.

Manchester, England, was the center of the world's cotton industry when Francis Cabot Lowell of Boston traveled there in 1811. The methods of making cotton cloth were very carefully guarded. No plans for machinery were available, and no drawings or note taking were permitted in the factories. But Lowell visited the factories and stored a multitude of details in his remarkable memory. When he returned to Waltham and established the Boston Manufacturing Company at Waltham, he was able to design all the necessary machinery entirely from memory. When opened in 1813, his was the first textile plant in America in which all operations from raw cotton to finished cloth were carried on under one roof. Francis Cabot Lowell is known as the father of American cotton manufacturing. Desiring to expand the Waltham operations, Lowell chose a site at the Pawtucket Falls on the Merrimac River in Lowell, named in his honor, where it could make full use of the water power.

The list of manufacturing firsts in Massachusetts is almost endless. The first machinery for sewing shoes was invented by Lyman Reed Blake of Abington. Massachusetts soon became the center of the American shoemaking industry. Today the USM Corporation at Beverly is the largest plant of its type in the world. Fourteen percent of all United States shoe production is in Massachusetts.

It is probable that a steam machine brought to Massachusetts was the first of any kind in the country, and this is now on display in the Dedham Historical Society Museum. The first practical machine for making envelopes was invented in 1852 by Russell Hawes of Worcester. Erastus Bigelow revolutionized rug making by inventing the first mechanical loom for carpets, at West Boylston. Ebenezer Butterick devised a new method of cutting and stamping patterns for dresses, and the popular, standardized dress pattern was born at Worcester.

The old furniture made by skilled craftsmen such as those at Salem is still prized. Gardner, where the Boston rocker was invented, was the early home of the chair making industry. It is claimed that the first friction matches made in the United States were produced at Chicopee, then part of Springfield. The Waltham Company studied the methods of manufacturing interchangeable parts developed by Eli Whitney and began to manufacture the first machine-made watches produced in America. In Boston the safety razor was invented and became so popular that the name of its inventor, Gillette, became a household word throughout the world.

Many cities of Massachusetts gained fame for their products.

Saugus Iron Works, sometimes called the "birthplace of American industry."

Sandwich glass is still among the most prized items of collectors. Greenfield produced the first cutlery made in America and is now home of the world's largest producer of taps and dies. Springfield is the industrial capital of western Massachusetts and is renowned as a source of firearms since before the Revolution. Ipswich was the first lace making town in the United States. The American hosiery industry was also born there.

Boston was for many years one of the greatest wool markets in the western world, and Peabody is a leading leather city. A center for paper making, especially the paper on which U.S. currency is printed, is Dalton, home of Crane and Company. Whitman has an unusual and tasty distinction. The famous Toll House cookies were created in the Toll House Inn there.

Cambridge is not generally known as a manufacturing center, but it has had many distinctions. At one time, before mechanical refrigeration, it controlled the ice industry. The country's first ladder factory was built there as well as a great carriage making plant. The first machines making galvanized iron pipe and piano keys were developed in Cambridge, along with flowerpots, reversible collars, mechanical egg beaters, and waterproof hats.

Lawrence sprang into being almost overnight as an industrial city, and the Connecticut River Valley is also known for its industry

51

Other famous companies in Massachusetts include Simonds Saw and Steel works in Fitchburg, noted for building one of the first of the now popular windowless factories. The Indian Motorcycle factory was at Springfield. One of the earliest industries, Towle Silversmiths of Newburyport, still flourishes. Lever Brothers once turned out enough soap at Cambridge to foam the globe.

The sound-test laboratory of General Electric Company at Dalton is known as the quietest room in the world. The General Electric Transformer Division experiments with machinery that produces the most powerful artificial lightning bolts ever generated. The original unit of this company at Lynn is still one of the largest private employers in the commonwealth. In fact, the electrical and related industries of Massachusetts employ more people than any other.

Aaron Dennison set up his manufacturing plant at Framingham, once noted for its novelties and party favors. When the New England Glass Company completed its huge 124-foot high (about 38 meters) chimney, they built a temporary platform and held a great banquet on its top to celebrate the completion.

Over three hundred Massachusetts companies are engaged in nuclear research, nucleonics, and atomic power, including the forty million dollar Yankee Atomic Energy Company power plant at Rowe. One of the first of the new, inexpensive electronic computers was developed by Mathatronics at Waltham. Route 128, a radial highway near Boston, is one of the biggest and fastest growing science-based locales in the United States.

Massachusetts is one of the leading states in the all-important field of research, with more than 320 research laboratories employing 21,000 scientists, engineers, and technicians.

Altogether, manufacturing in Massachusetts annually adds nearly twelve billion dollars to the commonwealth.

TRANSPORTATION AND COMMUNICATION

"Never, in these United States, has the brain of man conceived, or the hand of man fashioned, so perfect a thing as the clipper ship," wrote Samuel E. Morison in his *Maritime History of Massachusetts*. These fast, beautiful ships were among Massachusetts' greatest contributions to transportation. Names like the *Flying Cloud* and *Sovereign of the Seas* will remain among the most famous. In 1859 the clipper *Dreadnaught* was the marvel of the world with its record crossing of the Atlantic in nine days and thirteen hours.

However, Massachusetts built other famous ships besides the clippers. The *Blessing of the Bay,* the first ship built at Boston was launched in 1631. Our most famous warship, the United States frigate *Constitution,* was designed by Captain George Claghorn of Martha's Vineyard, and built by Edmund Hart. Bethlehem Steel at Quincy turned out the first nuclear-powered surface ship, the guided missile cruiser *Long Beach.*

As early as 1666 there were three hundred ships making port at Boston. Massachusetts was noted as the home of many captains. In Falmouth alone lived 148 sailing captains, their homes proudly marked with a golden eagle over the door. Today, Boston ranks among the top twenty saltwater ports of the United States.

One of the early canals in America was the Old Middlesex Canal, opened in 1803 by Loammi Baldwin, running 25 miles (about 40 kilometers) from Lowell to Somerville.

Land transportation in Massachusetts also has a notable history. The three routes of the old Boston Post Road are still well remembered. Over this route the first rider carried the post from Boston to New York in 1673. This was no speedy mail service, like the Pony Express of later days. The riders jogged along at such an easy pace that one rider generally knitted as he rode.

The Mohawk Trail was blazed by the Indians as a footpath, and taken over by the settlers as a road for oxen. In 1789, it became the first toll-free "interstate" road in America, known as a shunpike, because it shunned the many roads where travelers were forced to pay tolls to the private owners every few miles. Today the Mohawk Trail is one of the country's superb scenic highways.

Travel over the early roads was by stagecoach. It is interesting to know that they took this name because they traveled by stages, that is, an agreed upon number of miles a day, regardless of weather.

Frequently the passengers had to walk uphill or push the awkward vehicle out of the mud. Today's travelers skim across the state at the legal limit on such leading routes as the Massachusetts Turnpike and the many other modern highways of the commonwealth.

The "granite railroad" at Quincy was the first successful railroad in the United States. The Boston and Worcester railroad opened in 1835, and soon the state was covered with a network of railroads. One of the oldest railroad tunnels in the United States, the Hoosac, was drilled under Hoosac Mountain in the Berkshire Hills from 1851 to 1875. It is 4¾ miles (about 8 kilometers) long. In other rail fields, Massachusetts pioneered with the first electric powered street railroad, developed at Brockton, and America's first passenger subway opened at Boston around the turn of the century.

In modern public transportation, Massachusetts is determined to make Boston as great in overseas air commerce as its ocean ships once were. Logan International Airport is one of the nation's greatest, and has one of the longest runways. It is one of the few major commercial airports served by a rapid transit line.

In the field of communication, Massachusetts' people have pioneered many important advances. Samuel F.B. Morse, inventor of the telegraph and the Morse code, was born in Boston and developed his great invention there. The first telegraph line was built at Concord. The all-important telephone was invented by the Scotsman, Alexander Graham Bell, while he lived at Wellesley. Marconi's original wireless station was set up at Eastham.

At Cambridge, sponsored by Harvard College, Stephen Daye set up the first press in Massachusetts, and the first book ever published in the United States, the *Bay Psalm Book,* appeared in 1640. The first newspaper in the United States was the Boston *News Letter,* published in 1704.

AGRICULTURE

Usually agricultural products are not thought of as being invented, but Massachusetts has originated new types of products.

About half of America's cranberries are grown in Massachusetts.

The famous Concord grape was developed at Concord in 1853 by Ephraim Bull. Although this was the beginning of commercial development of table grapes in America, Bull did not make any great profit on his discovery. His tombstone reads "He sowed; others reaped." Today, the Concord grape is not grown commercially at its birthplace. Although the first vine was winterkilled, the present vine is a shoot from the original root.

The equally famous Baldwin apple was originated by Middlesex Canal developer, Loammi Baldwin, at Woburn. At the Baldwin mansion today are aged Baldwin trees descended from the original.

Renowned in song and poem, the Rambler rose was developed by Michael Walsh in 1893 at the Fay Rose Gardens near Falmouth. By contrast, the great Morgan strain of work horses originated at West Springfield.

Although agriculture has diminished in importance, Massachusetts still realizes a substantial annual income from farm marketing. The largest part of this is from dairy and poultry products. Carver is the largest cranberry producing center in the world, and 50 percent of all American cranberries are grown in Massachusetts. They are the leading agricultural product of Cape Cod.

In a most ambitious and imaginative business endeavor United Fruit Company of Boston turned the jungles of Central America and the Caribbean Islands into vast banana plantations, building model communities for workers, creating fleets of cargo ships, and building railroads. This has become one of the largest produce operations the world has ever known.

Contrasted with this are the many "kitchen industries" of Massachusetts, based on the wild and cultivated fruits and vegetables. Green Briar Jam Kitchen, using the wild fruits and berries of Cape Cod, is a good example of this kind of individual initiative.

FISHING AND WHALING

There is probably more romance and tragedy in the story of Massachusetts' fishing and whaling than in any other activity.

Codfish were the first settlers' initial export and source of revenue, and they are still of some importance. At one time, fishing was the region's greatest source of wealth. Massachusetts is fourth among all the states in commercial fishing, with a revenue of nearly $100,000,000 from fishing annually.

Gloucester continues to be one of the great fishing towns of the East Coast. During the more than three hundred years its men have

Gloucester commemorates its fishermen.

THEY THAT GO
DOWN TO THE SEA
IN SHIPS
· · ·
1623 — 1923

gone to the sea in fishing ships, 10,000 Gloucestermen have been lost at sea. The town holds an impressive annual service in their memory. All along the coast old houses may still be seen with their roof walks where anxious wives of fishermen would pace, peering seaward for their men's safe return.

The invention of the beam trawler in 1904 transformed the fishing practices of Gloucester and other fishing communities into something more like modern factory methods.

The American whaling industry began at Martha's Vineyard, where early settlers learned whaling from the Indians. Nantucket Island was the world's greatest whaling port from the late 1600s to the early 1800s. Then New Bedford became the leading whaling port. Herman Melville once remarked that the houses of New Bedford had been "dragged from the sea," meaning that as whales were pulled from the ocean they provided the wealth to build the town.

Soon after oil was discovered in Pennsylvania, in 1857, the whaling industry began to decline because the new oil was better, cheaper, and more easily obtained than whale oil. For a time New Bedford almost became a ghost town when its great whaling fleet was scrapped.

MINERAL AND TIMBER ACTIVITIES

One of the greatest modern industries in the world, the American steel industry, had its start in Massachusetts when in 1656 the mill at Taunton manufactured the first iron ever produced in factory quantities in the United States. Iron production continued in Massachusetts until 1922. Great quantities of iron and steel are used in Massachusetts industry, but these are brought in from other states.

New England's first mine was opened in 1640 near Sturbridge to produce graphite, but the effort failed. There are substantial coal deposits, but the principal minerals in production today are stone, sand, gravel, lime, and clays. The annual mineral production in Massachusetts is about sixty million dollars.

Much commercial timber is harvested in Massachusetts each year.

Louisa May Alcott School of Philosophy in Concord.

Human Treasures

CREATIVE GENIUS

More of America's greatest cultural geniuses have come from Massachusetts than from any other area. Some claim that the total of great literary and artistic names of Massachusetts would equal that of all the other states put together. So outstanding is Massachusetts in this regard that it is fondly known as custodian of America's cultural heritage.

The years 1830 through 1880 saw a great literary flowering centered in and near Boston. The period was amazing because of the number of great writers and thinkers who lived in those years, most of them close enough to associate with one another regularly. Not the greatest author, but certainly the most commanding figure of the period, was Ralph Waldo Emerson. Born in Boston and educated at Harvard, he left the ministry to become a writer. Through much of his long life (1803-1882), he was acknowledged as the dean of American philosophers and leader of the group of Massachusetts' writers.

His friend Henry David Thoreau, 1817-1862, a native of Concord, was best known for his classic work *Walden.* He was very fond of Cape Cod and described a walking trip the length of the Cape in his work *Cape Cod,* which sometimes shows his humorous and human side. He describes his visit at the home of a Wellfleet oysterman, who was constantly spitting a broad stream of tobacco juice into the fireplace while his wife prepared breakfast: "I ate of the apple-sauce and the doughnuts, which I thought had sustained the least detriment from the old man's shots, but my companion refused the apple-sauce and ate of the hot cake and green beans, which had appeared to him to occupy the safest part of the hearth."

It has been said that the only "genuine artist" of this golden age of letters was Nathaniel Hawthorne, born in Salem in 1804, dying in 1864. However, another critic says that "without any question the greatest book which has come out of New England and one of the greatest works of prose fiction ever written in any language is *Moby*

Dick, by Herman Melville, written at his home, Arrowhead, at Pittsfield. In spite of his friendship with Hawthorne, the greatness of Melville's work was not generally recognized until long after his death in 1891.

Another writer who received almost no recognition during his short lifetime was Boston-born Edgar Allan Poe, 1809-1849. His work was long admired in Europe, but only in rather recent years has Poe been acknowledged as one of America's greatest literary geniuses. One of Poe's stories, *The Cask of Amontillado,* tells of a man being sealed alive behind a brick wall. When he was eighteen, Poe served in the army at Fort Independence, Boston. In 1905, by strange coincidence, a skeleton in army uniform was found behind a wall when a part of the fort was torn down.

Fortunately, not all the writers had to wait until after their deaths to be acclaimed. One of the most widely recognized men of letters during his lifetime was the poet Henry Wadsworth Longfellow, 1807-1882, not born in Massachusetts, but a professor at Harvard.

Another of Massachusetts' literary greats was Oliver Wendell Holmes, born at Cambridge in 1809. He was also noted as a physician, and his medical papers have considerable importance. His son, Oliver Wendell Holmes, Jr., served on the United States Supreme Court for thirty years.

Massachusetts claims many other writers: poets Eugene Field, whose boyhood home was Amherst; William Cullen Bryant, who practiced law at Great Barrington; John Greenleaf Whittier, born at Haverhill; and Samuel Smith of Andover who wrote "My Country 'tis of Thee"—which has become our national hymn, *America.*

Massachusetts women have been among the most notable writers. Emily Dickinson spent practically all of her life at Amherst. She rarely visited with people and lived almost in seclusion. Not until several years after her death did she begin to be recognized as one of the leading women poets of all time. Amy Lowell, the cigar smoking poetess of Brookline, lived a life almost completely different from Emily Dickenson. Among the best-loved women writers of Massachusetts is Louisa May Alcott of Concord, author of *Little Women* and *Little Men.*

Among more recent writers associated with Massachusetts are Hamlin Garland, who came to Boston from the Dakotas and for a time lived on forty cents a day; William Dean Howells; William James; Conrad Aiken; and T.S. Eliot. Not considered a great writer, but remarkable for the success and quantity of his books, was Horatio Alger of Revere, who published 119 works.

One of the great poets of modern times, Robert Frost, spent his later life in Massachusetts, where he died in 1963. The first plays of Eugene O'Neill were staged by the Provincetown Players.

PUBLIC FIGURES

Three native sons and one adopted son of Massachusetts have been elected to the presidency of the United States—John Adams, John Quincy Adams, Calvin Coolidge, and John Fitzgerald Kennedy.

Abigail and John Adams, painted by Benjamin Blythe.

John Fitzgerald Kennedy was born in Brookline, and educated in Dexter, Riverdale Country Day, Canterbury, Choate, Princeton, Harvard, London School of Economics, and Stanford.

Kennedy's political career began in 1947 when he was elected congressman from Massachusetts. Six years later he became U.S. senator. In 1956, he failed to win the Democratic nomination for Vice-President, but he received so much attention that in 1960 he won the Democratic nomination for the presidency. He defeated the Republican candidate, Richard M. Nixon, to become the thirty-fifth President of the United States.

President Kennedy's family has long had an active interest in both local and national politics. His father, Joseph P. Kennedy, after amassing a huge fortune, became ambassador to England under President Franklin Delano Roosevelt. Although he never held an elective office, Joseph Kennedy maintained his active interest in politics and inspired his three sons, John, Robert, and Edward, to continue the family's tradition of public service.

Robert Kennedy served as Attorney General under his brother. In 1964 he won his first elective office, and became senator from New York. His brother, Edward, was elected to a second term as senator from Massachusetts in the same year.

The good fortune of wealth, personal charm, and high position of the Kennedy family has been marred by a recurring element of tragedy. This tragic element reached its climax on November 22, 1963, when President Kennedy was assassinated, and continued when Robert Kennedy was assassinated in 1968.

Only one father and son team ever has occupied the White House. These were members of Massachusetts' Adams family of Quincy. As second President of the United States, John Adams found following the great George Washington a difficult and often thankless task. In those days the Vice-President was not necessarily of the same political party. Thomas Jefferson, Vice-President under Adams, opposed the president and increased John Adams' troubles. Strangely, both of those men died on the same day—the Fourth of July—in 1826. Adams was ninety-one years old.

John Quincy Adams had a brilliant career of public service. He helped negotiate the treaty of peace after the War of 1812, served as American minister to the Netherlands, and as a senator from Massachusetts. He became the sixth President of the United States in 1825. Neither he nor his father could win election to second terms. However, after his defeat for reelection, John Quincy Adams became a congressman from Massachusetts and served nine terms. He died in 1848 after suffering a stroke on the floor of the House.

Calvin Coolidge was born in Vermont, but most of his career of public service occurred in Massachusetts, and his forefathers arrived with the founders of Boston in 1630. He became President upon the death of President Warren G. Harding, and was elected in his own right in 1924. When the Republican party was eager to nominate him once more, he declared, "I do not choose to run."

He retired from the presidency to his home, the Beeches, where he died in 1933.

The great Benjamin Franklin was born in Boston on January 17, 1706, and his mother brought him to the old South Church to be baptized on the same day. He served in his brother's print shop in Boston, but his famous career occurred after he had left the commonwealth.

Other notable careers of public service include those of the renowned orator, Massachusetts Senator Edward Everett, who also was president of Harvard University; Henry Wilson, vice-president of the United States from 1873 to 1875; and Henry Cabot Lodge, United States senator from Massachusetts and ambassador to the United Nations under President Dwight Eisenhower.

ARTISTS, ARCHITECTS, SCULPTORS

The first artist of the United States to gain great fame was Gilbert Stuart, noted chiefly for his portraits of George Washington, who settled in Massachusetts. James Abbott McNeill Whistler, considered by some to be America's greatest artist, was born in Lowell, although much of his career was carried on outside the United States. The same is true of the artist Winslow Homer. Samuel F.B.

Morse is not usually thought of as an artist, yet his success as the inventor of the telegraph and Morse code never consoled him for giving up his very promising career in art. His fine self-portrait may still be seen at the Addison Gallery in Andover.

Possibly the most awe-inspiring and most looked at work of art in the world is the magnificent seated statue of Lincoln, the only object to occupy the Lincoln Memorial. This is the work of Daniel Chester French of Glendale, who also created the *Minuteman* at Concord. Henry Hudson Kitson did his work at Tyringham. His *Minuteman* at Lexington and his *Puritan Maid* at Plymouth are also very well known.

The nation's first professional architect was Charles Bulfinch. His fine buildings which still stand in Massachusetts are eagerly sought out by all admirers of fine architecture. The State House at Boston is one of his outstanding structures. Other Massachusetts' architects are Samuel McIntyre of Salem, known as the master builder, and Isaac Damon, famous both as an architect and builder of bridges.

SUCH INTERESTING PEOPLE

Beginning with the Pilgrims, the list of interesting Massachusetts people is almost endless. Such familiar names as Myles Standish, Edward Winslow, Elder Brewster, and Governor William Bradford come to mind at once. Governor Bradford was elected thirty times, and it has been said that the Pilgrims could not have managed without him.

The early people of Massachusetts loved puns and they used to say they had cotton for their clothing, hooker for their fishing and stone for building, referring to the leaders John Cotton, Thomas Hooker, and Samuel Stone. The contribution of such men as Governor John Winthrop of the Massachusetts Bay Colony cannot be overlooked. It was he who insisted that the new colony must govern itself and be free of control from England. Possibly this more than any other one thing led to democracy in America.

A hardy pioneer in the truest sense of the word was sturdy Hannah

Paul Revere's statue stands in Paul Revere Mall. The Old North Church is in the background.

Dustin. In March, 1697, she was abducted by the Indians, but later she and two other captives fought so fiercely that they escaped, carrying back with them the scalps of ten Indian captors.

Paul Revere (his Huguenot name is Rivoire) is little known for his many accomplishments other than his midnight ride. However, he was a fine silversmith, and many of his excellent pieces are highly prized today. He was one of the early manufacturers, casting bells of good quality, some of which are still in use. He was a pioneer in the manufacture of false teeth. These he made, naturally enough, from silver. An old advertisement for his dentures claimed they were "of real use in speaking and eating."

Three other men should have reputations equal with Revere's as messengers of the Revolution: William Dawes, Dr. Samuel Prescott, and Israel Bissell, who has been called the unsung Paul Revere. Bissell made a heroic ride, galloping for five days to carry the news of Lexington through Connecticut, New York, and clear to Philadelphia.

Probably no other state can claim so many founders and improvers of religious institutions. These names include Jonathan Edwards, Dwight L. Moody, William Ellery Channing, and Mary Baker Eddy.

Northampton minister Jonathan Edwards was responsible for the first great religious revival in America, known as the Great Awakening. His preaching drove all of New England into a frenzied terror of hellfire. When Edwards was forced to retire from Northampton, he went to preach and teach as a missionary among the Stockbridge Indians. There he wrote his famous work *On the Freedom of Will.*

Dwight Lyman Moody, born in Northfield, was the son of a poor widow. After he became financially successful he was converted to Christianity, and brought about another great revival movement in America. He founded the famous Student Volunteer Movement to bring young people into foreign missionary work. Such great churches as Moody Church, the Moody Bible Institute in Chicago, Illinois, and the Moody Science Institute in California are evidences of the far-reaching influence of Moody's work.

William Ellery Channing guided the new Unitarian movement in its sweep through the commonwealth.

One of the world's most notable women and one of the most influential in history was Mary Baker Eddy. Mary Baker had been in poor health since childhood. Her study of health problems resulted in her profound belief of healing through religious conviction.

She began her demonstrations of healing as early as 1866. Her renowned statement of the principles of her faith, *Science and Health with Key to the Scriptures,* was published in 1875. This work developed into the Church of Christ Scientist, founded by Mary Baker Eddy in 1879. The worldwide operation of this church and all its many activities, such as publishing, are the direct result of her untiring and dedicated efforts. When she was 87 she founded the international daily newpaper, the *Christian Science Monitor.*

Other Massachusetts' healers were Dorothea L. Dix, who was America's pioneer in the care and restoration of the mentally ill, and Clara Barton, founder of the American Red Cross. Four other notable Massachusetts' women were Susan B. Anthony, pioneer in women's rights; Emily Post of Edgartown, who was long the nation's leader in manners and social customs; Maria Mitchell, born on Nantucket Island, who was America's first woman astronomer; and Elizabeth Poole of Taunton, pioneer woman industrialist.

Black leaders of Massachusetts include one of the martyrs of the Revolution, Crispus Attucks. He was a runaway slave and was killed in the Boston Massacre, and is sometimes considered the first casualty of the American Revolution.

Boston dentist William T.G. Morton first demonstrated the use of ether as an anaesthetic in a surgical operation at Massachusetts General Hospital in 1846. Peter Parker established the first modern hospital in China. Donald B. MacMillan of Provincetown was one of the leading Arctic explorers.

A man known as the first great United States philanthropist was George Peabody, in whose honor a Massachusetts city was named. He began life as a poor boy and made a great fortune in London as a banker. He refused an offer of knighthood by Queen Victoria and accepted instead a small miniature portrait of the queen from her own hands. This miniature is now on exhibit at the Peabody Institute in Salem. When he died, funeral services were held in Westminster Abbey, and the queen's greatest warship brought his body back home to the United States for burial. He donated funds to create schools, museums, and other living institutions not only in Massachusetts but throughout the country.

Other business leaders include Linus Yale, who made his first Yale locks at Shelburne; Peter Faneuil, who donated the famous Boston hall bearing his name; Andrew W. Preston of United Fruit Company; and Stephen Van Rensselaer of Woburn, promoter of the Erie Canal.

When John Quincy Adams failed to get the electoral votes to make him President, the decision was thrown to the House of Representatives. When Van Rensselaer, then a member of Congress, came to choose, he closed his eyes and prayed. Opening his eyes he saw the name John Q. Adams on a ballot at his feet. His vote for Adams was the deciding one.

Memorial Church, built in the 1930s, stands near the center of Harvard's campus.

Teaching and Learning

The educational values of the United States had their beginnings in Massachusetts. If only one of the great contributions of the commonwealth to our culture and well-being could be selected, the pattern and tradition of education would have to be selected as foremost.

The people of Massachusetts on the average complete more years of schooling than any others. The concentration of over thirty degree-granting institutions in the greater Boston area unquestionably makes this one of the world's most influential centers of learning. It is interesting to note that 50 percent of the graduates of this region remain in the area to carry on their life work.

Since 1635 Massachusetts has achieved more firsts in education than any other state. Only five years after they came to this country, still surrounded by wilderness, the Puritans took two of the most significant steps in our history: They established the country's first public school in 1635, and laid the beginnings for the first university in the following year.

Four hundred English pounds amounted to a large sum of money, more than the annual income of the colony, when the Massachusetts Bay Colony General Court appropriated that sum to start a college at Newtowne, later Cambridge. Its aim was to educate English and Indian youth in knowledge and Godliness. This is said to be the first body in which the people, by their representatives, ever gave their own money to found a place of education.

The young minister, John Harvard, had not been too well liked because of his advanced ideas, but on his death in 1638 it was found that he had willed his entire estate—1700 pounds in money and a fine library of books—to the new college. Opinions about John Harvard quickly changed, and his name was given to the infant institution.

The first years were not easy for Harvard. Its teachers were sometimes paid in grain or wampum. Part of the president's salary was paid in the form of a goat, which promptly died. One student wrote "a great many bears are killed at Cambridge."

Harvard's benefactor, John Harvard, is remembered in this famous bronze in the Harvard University Yard.

Today, except at the museum, the bears are gone, and that struggling institution has become the wealthiest university in the world and one of the most important. It has graduated more United States Presidents than any other; both Adamses, both Roosevelts, and John F. Kennedy.

Too many important discoveries have been made there and too many important professors and graduates have been associated with Harvard to list them here, but its influence has been enormous.

In Cambridge, however, Harvard must share educational honors with the more recent Massachusetts Institute of Technology, also one of the world's leading institutions. In a most colorful ceremony, M.I.T. moved from Copley Square to its Charles River campus in 1916. A solemn procession carried a gilded chest to the water's edge on the Boston side. In the chest were the institute's charter and other important papers. The chest was carefully placed on a Venetian barge and rowed across the Charles to its new home while thousands watched and cheered. Among the innumerable awards recognizing the institute or its faculty was the 1964 Nobel Prize in physics, awarded to Dr. Charles Towne of the faculty for his work in the development of the maser and laser.

Colleges for women have flowered in Massachusetts. Mary Lyon pioneered in this field at Mt. Holyoke, established at South Hadley in 1836. Wellesley College is noted especially for the work of Alice Freeman Palmer. Sophia Smith founded the college bearing her name at Northampton in 1875. Radcliffe College, begun in 1879, was named for Ann Radcliffe, the first woman to endow a scholarship at Harvard.

The first and second state teachers' colleges in the country were established at Lexington and Westfield. The University of Massachusetts at Amherst was founded in 1863.

Space will not permit mention here of the many other outstanding colleges and universities of Massachusetts, but a complete list can be found in reference works.

It is incredible to realize that as early as 1647 Massachusetts had a law requiring establishment of an elementary school in all towns of fifty families and also a secondary school in all towns of over one hundred families. In 1639, the Mather School of Boston became the first free public school. The first free public school in America supported by taxation was established at Dedham in 1649.

Massachusetts has a long list of distinguished private schools, including Groton, school of Franklin D. Roosevelt; Roxbury Latin School, oldest private secondary school in the United States; Mt. Hermon School for Boys and Northfield School for girls, both founded by Dwight L. Moody; and Phillips Academy for boys, at Andover. This is the oldest boys' boarding school in the country, and was described in the poem "The School Boy" by Oliver Wendell Holmes. One of Massachusetts' most famous schools does not even have a name. This is the schoolhouse at Sudbury mentioned in the well-loved poem about Mary and her little lamb.

Education, not only in Massachusetts, but throughout the world owes a debt to one of the greatest of all educators—Horace Mann, born at Franklin. Horace Mann was influential in spreading the belief that everyone deserves the best possible education, and for making the world realize the importance of education.

The skyline of downtown Boston from the Charles River.

Enchantment of Massachusetts

THE HUB OF THE UNIVERSE

The people of Boston have never been content to be the "hub of the earth." They strive to make their metropolis—and have always considered that it was—the "hub of the universe," as it was called by Oliver Wendell Holmes. He also added humorously that even the flowers and shrubs of the entire metropolitan area inclined their heads toward Boston Common. This attraction is apparently shared by the people, since the Boston metropolitan section is the third most densely populated area in the nation.

It is frequently said that greater Boston is a fascinating combination of old and new, but it is the region's history that holds most interest for visitors. Both local and Federal governments are currently developing a complex of National Historic sites in the Boston area.

These include: Faneuil Hall, Cradle of American Liberty, with its famed grasshopper weathervane; the Old State House; Shirley-Eustis House; Paul Revere House; Old North Church; Bunker Hill; and Dorchester Heights National Historic Site.

The Old State House has stood at the head of State Street since 1748. The first public reading of the Declaration of Independence in Boston occurred on its balcony. A circle of cobblestones in the pavement below marks the place where the Boston Massacre heralded a revolution. One of the favorite Boston memorials of this event is the statue of Crispus Attucks, black revolutionary killed in the massacre.

Paul Revere's home is supposed to be the oldest frame house still standing in Boston, and the Old North Church, where the lantern in the tower signaled Paul, is the oldest church in the city.

The Bunker Hill monument, commemorating the battle of June 17, 1775, is one of the most familiar in America. Dorchester Heights National Historic Site recalls the part played by the American batteries of cannon brought to Boston with such great labor. These helped drive the British from the city.

One of the most popular tourist attractions in the nation is the historic American naval ship the *U.S.S. Constitution,* but more popularly known as *Old Ironsides.* It was launched in 1797, carried forty-four guns and weighed 1,576 tons (about 1,430 metric tons).

It earned its nickname in battle with the British warship *Guerrier,* when it turned aside so many cannonballs its sides seemed to be made of iron. The ship was condemned to be broken up in 1830, but Oliver Wendell Holmes published his thrilling poem "Old Ironsides," and the public demanded that the precious relic be saved. Rebuilt, it served as a training ship until 1877. In 1927, with an avalanche of pennies from school children and other contributions, *Old Ironsides* was restored and permanently anchored in Boston harbor.

Few cities in America have been selected as the final resting place for so many famous people. Most of the prominent Bostonians of the past hundred years were buried at Mt. Auburn Cemetery, including Mary Baker Eddy, Oliver Wendell Holmes, James Russell Lowell, Henry Wadsworth Longfellow, Charles Sumner, Louis Agassiz, Edwin Booth, Phillips Brooks, William Ellery Channing, and Julia Ward Howe. The Old Granary Burial Ground contains graves of Peter Faneuil, John Hancock, Paul Revere, Samuel Adams, victims of the Boston Massacre, and many others.

Many of these famous people gathered at the Old Corner Book Store, one of Boston's oldest brick buildings. The notables apt to drop in there included Longfellow, Hawthorne, Emerson, Holmes, Harriet Beecher Stowe, and others responsible for Boston's Golden Age of Letters.

The present Capitol building of Massachusetts, the State House, with its handsome golden dome, was built in 1795-98 and is con-

The Capitol in Boston.

sidered the masterpiece of the master architect, Charles Bulfinch. Bulky wings were added later. Inside are the Hall of Flags, the seals of the original thirteen states, the renowned Sacred Cod, the original charter of the Massachusetts Bay Colony, 1628, and the original copy of the Massachusetts constitution of 1780. Facing the State House is Augustus St. Gauden's noted monument showing Colonel Robert Gould Shaw leading his black regiment in the Civil War.

Boston is the home of the Mother Church of Christian Science, seating 5,000 people, and of the Christian Science Publishing House. This latter contains the famed "Maparium," an illuminated globe of the world so huge, visitors walk into it as in a room. This is headquarters for one of the world's most renowned newspapers, the *Christian Science Monitor.*

In today's Boston, the Roman Catholic faith has the largest number of followers, an interesting contrast to the Protestant beginnings of the city. One of its splendid and well-known edifices is the Cathedral of the Holy Cross, completed in 1875 after seven years of labor.

Typical of the dynamic rebuilding Boston is undertaking is the mammoth center around the fifty-two story Prudential Building. The 32-acre (about 12.9 hectares) Back Bay site is a major office and convention headquarters. A thousand-room hotel, large convention and exhibition hall, seventy-five retail shops, a skating rink, and spacious plazas add to the usefulness of the area. It rivals Rockefeller Plaza in New York City in importance.

The old Scollay Square area has been transformed into a dramatic government center, with City Hall, the John F. Kennedy Federal Building, and a complex of state office buildings.

Education and literature are only two of the fields that give Boston its reputation as one of the world's leading cultural centers. Music, art, and museums continue to be outstanding.

Boston has long been one of the foremost musical centers of the country. America's first native composer of music was William Billings, composer of the *New England Psalm Singer.* George Chadwick, Walter Piston, and Roger Sessions are the outstanding Massachusetts composers of modern times. The first pipe organ in America was installed in King's Chapel in 1714; Handel's *Messiah* was given in its entirety at Boston as early as 1818. The New England Conservatory of Music, founded 1867, became one of the most famous music schools. The great Boston Symphony was begun in 1881, largely through the generosity and devotion of Lee Higginson. Its conductors have included such first-rank leaders as Pierre Montieux and Serge Koussevitzky. Symphony Hall is said to rate among the best of all concert halls in its acoustics. The concerts of the Boston Pops orchestra are known around the world. In summer they are given in Hatch Memorial Shell on the Esplanade.

The Boston Museum of Art is especially noted for its fine collection of Far Eastern art. Isabella S. Gardner Museum has one of the finest of all Italian art collections. Among the few really extensive science museums anywhere is the Museum of Science and Hayden Planetarium in Science Park. One of the books in the Athenaeum, the biography of an outlaw, has a binding made from his own skin. This great library began with the private library of George Washington, purchased after his death. Among the largest library collections in the world is that of the Boston Public Library, offering the wealth of more than four million volumes. It is generally recognized as one of the great libraries of the United States.

Notable Boston parks include the Public Garden, where the famous swan boats silently glide by. The park is noted for its rare trees, formal gardens, and winter skating. Boston Common was established as a cow pasture and training ground. By law it is still available for those uses. Here at one time men were whipped at whipping posts or taunted in stocks for their crimes. Here, too, pirates and Quakers were hanged and trenches were dug to bury the British soldiers killed at Breed's Hill. Today, Boston Common is still a place where all may air their thoughts publicly.

Other places of interest in Boston include Beacon Hill, named for a beacon placed there in 1634; Louisburg Square; the Old South Church, with hand-carved pews designed to squeak so no one could slip in late; Park Street Church, where *America* was first sung; and Massachusetts General Hospital, where anesthesia was first used and where Oliver Wendell Holmes was a staff member.

GREATER BOSTON AREA

One of American industry's most notable shrines is the Saugus ironworks. This birthplace of the steel industry, has been restored by the Steel Institute, and is today an exciting piece of living United States history.

Greater Boston was the nineteenth century cultural center of the United States. In some ways, although other cultural centers now flourish, Cambridge still retains that leadership, through Massachusetts Institute of Technology and Harvard. Almost every visitor to Harvard looks for at least two attractions—the Yard, the oldest section of the campus, and the glass flowers of the botanical museum. No one has ever equaled the artistry of the German glass craftsman, Blaschka, who made this internationally renowned collection of delicate glass flowers.

At Cambridge may still be seen the house used by George Washington as his headquarters and later occupied by poet Henry Wadsworth Longfellow. The setting of Longfellow's poem, *The Village Blacksmith,* may also be found here.

The historic village green at Lexington is still much as it used to be. A lesser-known shrine of the Revolution is the Andrew Hall house at Medford, where Paul Revere made his first stop. The Barnum Museum in Medford was filled with a collection of the colorful showman's curiosities, but it burned.

Lincoln Village is noteworthy because of the number of unusual bequests that have been made to the community. One of these was to help local farmers find recreation. This is now used for fireworks on the Fourth of July. Another gift was to aid the silent poor; however, no one in Lincoln will admit to being poor. Julian de Cordova willed his estate and fine art collection to Lincoln along with a million dollars for maintenance. Lincoln is one of the smallest towns with such a fine museum, but in spite of the endowment, the upkeep is heavy for such a small community.

At Waltham is Brandeis University, founded in 1947. It is the first non-sectarian university of Jewish origin in the United States. The first American flag of thirteen stripes was flown at Somerville.

Watertown is the home of the noted Perkins Institution for the Blind. Perkins Institute and Massachusetts School for the Blind was founded in 1829, opened in South Boston in 1832, and removed to Watertown in 1912. Its first director was Dr. Samuel Gridley Howe. Dr. Howe dedicated his efforts to the emancipation of the deaf and the blind and, with the financial assistance of Thomas H. Perkins, the Perkins Institution and Massachusetts School for the Blind was founded, a unique institution for its day. Dr. Howe was assisted by his wife, Julia Ward Howe, the abolitionist, best known now as the author of "The Battle Hymn of the Republic."

Today, a general education from kindergarten through high school is offered, with emphasis on arts and crafts. A Braille library of 25,000 volumes is used in the school with free circulation among the blind in New England.

Fairbanks Homestead National Historic Site is at Dedham. This is said to be the oldest frame house still standing in America. Also at Dedham the Suffolk Resolves were born. Another National Historic Site is the Adams mansion at Quincy, home of two Presidents and many generations of the family. It was presented to the United States by the family in 1946.

A typical New England church in Lexington.

Made famous by Longfellow in *Tales of a Wayside Inn,* the Wayside Inn at Sudbury is the United States' oldest operating inn. At Wellesley, named for Samuel Welles, is the home of Mary Sawyer, supposed to be the Mary of "Mary had a little lamb" fame. Blackstone is the site of an unusual church. Half of the congregation sit in Massachusetts during a worship service; the other half sit in Rhode Island.

THE SOUTHEAST

Few towns in the United States fill the visitor with such a feeling of the past as Massachusetts' first settlement—Plymouth. It matters little whether the story of the Plymouth Rock is true or not. Lying under its marble canopy, it provides a magnificent reminder of those early adventurers. Other reminders are all about: the memorial sarcophagus on Coles Hill, containing the bones of early settlers; Burial Hill with its sad Pilgrim memories; the impressive National Monument to the Forefathers; and the Chief Massasoit statue.

Many reproductions show how the Pilgrims lived. The *Mayflower II* floats at anchor, welcoming more visitors in a few minutes than were in the first historic party. Pilgrim Village and Plymouth Plantation, with costumed attendants, show life as it was in 1627.

At South Carver, visitors are taken on a tour of the world's largest cranberry plantation on the Edaville Railroad, the only two-foot (about .6 meters), narrow-gauge passenger railroad now operating in the country.

Taunton makes two unusual claims. First, it is the largest city in Massachusetts in terms of area covered, stretching for 50 square miles (about 130 square kilometers) around the town green. Second, it also claims to be the cradle of American liberty. This claim is based on the fact that in 1774, a 112-foot (about 34 meters) Liberty Pole was raised on the green with a flag bearing the words "Liberty and Union, Union and Liberty."

One of the most notable buildings in the country, the Fall River City Hall, is built on air rights over Interstate Highway 195.

Memories of New Bedford's whaling greatness are preserved in its Whaling Museum. Particularly interesting there is the collection of scrimshaw (carved whales' teeth). Collecting scrimshaw was a favorite hobby of President John F. Kennedy. New Bedford's large Portuguese population each year faithfully carries on "The Crowning," a traditional ceremony of their native land. The Seamen's Bethel at New Bedford has a part in the great Herman Melville novel about the whale, *Moby Dick*.

THE CAPE AND THE ISLANDS

Massachusetts' fishhook in the Atlantic, Cape Cod, is noted as one of the world's prime resort areas. Parts of this region are still much as they have been since humans first saw them. "A man may stand and put all America behind him," as Thoreau said.

Five thousand acres (about 2,000 hectares) of the spectacular sand dunes and a total of almost 40,000 acres (about 16,000 hectares) of this wonderful natural treasure are being preserved or restored for all time in the Cape Cod National Seashore recreational area, created in 1961.

Provincetown is squeezed onto the Cape, 4 miles (about 6.4 kilometers) long and two streets wide. Here the Pilgrims' first landing in the New World is commemorated by the mighty 255-foot (about 69 meters) granite shaft of the Pilgrim Monument, a copy of the Torre del Mangia in Siena, Italy. There is also a Pilgrim museum. Also in tribute to the Pilgrims at Provincetown is a tablet commemorating the five who died on the long hard voyage.

Provincetown is one of the best preserved colonial towns in America. Visitors are intrigued by the town crier, who still makes his rounds. The town has been a leader in art and theater. Charles Hawthorne, an art teacher, founded the famous Provincetown bohemian art and literary colony. Provincetown Theater is known as the birthplace of the American theater. Another notable Provincetown museum is the Historical Museum, featuring the collection of the noted Arctic explorer from Provincetown, Donald B. MacMillan.

A street scene in Provincetown.

The Portuguese colony of Provincetown has many colorful feast days and religious processions.

Sandwich was the first town established on the Cape. It became one of the principal glassworking centers and was renowned for its beautiful art glassware, much of it preserved in the Glass Museum. A gristmill of 1654, the Hoxie House, oldest on Cape Cod, and a church spire by Christopher Wren, who designed St. Paul's Cathedral in London, are Sandwich landmarks.

The Bourne museum boasts the largest ship model in the world. Aptuxcet Trading Post there was probably the first of its kind in America. President Grover Cleveland maintained his summer White House at Bourne. Bourndale was the site of the first Indian church established by the Plymouth colony. Barnstable has the oldest library building in America (1645).

Falmouth was the birthplace of Katherine Lee Bates, author of

81

"America the Beautiful." The Congregational Church there has a bell cast by Paul Revere. Craigville Beach at Hyannisport is called one of the famous beaches of the world, and Nauset one of the most spectacular ocean beaches on the Atlantic.

Monomoy Shoals off Chatham was a favorite location for "moon cussing." This was the colorful name given to the despicable custom of luring ships to their doom with false lights and then looting the wrecked vessels. A famous Cape wreck was that of Pirate Sam Belamy near Wellfleet. A hundred and one buccaneers were drowned.

Chatham has two interesting museums: the railroad museum and the Shaker Museum, a collection of 7,000 items associated with the Shaker people. One of the Cape's most interesting communities is Woods Hole. Its three major organizations are the National Fisheries Service Laboratory, the Marine Biological Laboratory, and Woods Hole Oceanographic Institute. (The oldest Indian church in the eastern United States is at Mashpee in Barnstable County.)

Off Cape Cod are interesting pieces of land. *Moby Dick's* opening scenes were laid on Nantucket Island; Main Street there is said to be one of the most beautiful in New England. Many of the lovely homes are called whale oil mansions, because they were built from the wealth from whaling. There is a whaling museum on the island.

Shakespeare may have taken his *The Tempest* from a description of Martha's Vineyard by Gosnold. On this island are Massachusetts' only Indian settlements of today. At Gay Head the Indians sell pottery, made from local clay, and other wares.

THE NORTHEAST

Records of the infamous witch trials may still be seen in the courthouse at Salem, and the Corwin House (Witch House) still stands. Exhibits of pioneer life are shown at Essex Institute, in the reproduction of a waterfront thoroughfare of the Salem Maritime National Historic Site, and in Pioneer Village. At Salem are Hawthorne's "House of Seven Gables" and Peabody Museum.

Marblehead is one of the noted yachting centers of the world. The original painting "Spirit of '76" hangs in Abbott Hall in Marblehead.

Captains Courageous by Kipling was a tale of the Gloucester fishing fleet, which is remembered in the Fisherman's Memorial. There the first Universalist Church in the United States was established.

Rockport is said to have the only municipally owned artist's model in the world. The little red fish house on the wharf is perhaps the most often-painted object in the country. In order to preserve this landmark, the people of Rockport held a town meeting and voted to buy it.

Famed residents of Lowell have included the artist James McNeill Whistler and John Lowell, Jr., who gave a fortune to establish the Lowell Institute. John Greenleaf Whittier's birthplace near Haverhill and Merrimac has been restored. This was the setting for his famous poem *Snowbound.*

Concord was named for an agreement or concord with the Indians. Minuteman National Historical Park features the Minuteman statue by Daniel Chester French. Concord is known as the great literary shrine where many Massachusetts authors wrote; Emerson, Thoreau, and Hawthorne are buried in Sleepy Hollow Cemetery there. The Emerson home at Concord was the setting for Hawthorne's *Mosses from an Old Manse.*

Many of the great names of Concord took part in the Brook Farm experiment in West Roxbury. This was an early attempt at communal living where all shared the work and the enjoyments. After a good many discouragements, the Utopian plan was abandoned.

CENTRAL MASSACHUSETTS

The site of Worcester was purchased from the Indians by Dan Gookin for twelve pounds, two coats, and four yards (about 3.7 meters) of cloth. Today, the city is noted for its institutions, including the College of the Holy Cross and Worcester Polytechnic Institute. The Worcester Art Museum is one of the finest in the country and the Higgins Armory Museum among the best.

One of the few really extensive and qualified reproductions is that of old Sturbridge Village. This recreated colonial village covering 200 acres (about 81 hectares) brings together 23 buildings, about half of them original structures from their first sites. They include gun,

Sturbridge Village.

optical, cabinet, blacksmith, and other shops, mills, stores, and a school. There are exhibits and demonstrations of colonial handicraft.

CONNECTICUT VALLEY

Springfield was the site of the first United States arsenal. Today it has five major museums, possibly a record for a city of its size. Among these are the Smith Art Museum, museum of science, planetarium, and Museum of Fine Arts. Trinity Methodist Church is renowned for its twenty-four stained glass windows and carillon of sixty-one bells. The Eastern States Exposition at Springfield is said to be the biggest agricultural fair in the East.

Northampton was the home of Calvin Coolidge. After he retired from the White House, he bought The Beeches at Northampton, where he died. The view from the top of Mt. Holyoke near Northampton is considered one of the finest panoramas in New England.

Deerfield claims to have the most beautiful residential street in America. The first youth hostel in this country was founded at Northfield in 1934. Not far from Northfield, the French King Bridge over the Connecticut River has been cited as one of the most beautiful in the hemisphere. Another unusual bridge is the bridge of flowers at Shelburne Falls, almost covered with flowers and vines.

THE WEST — BUT NOT WILD

The Red Mill near Sheffield has been in operation for over two hundred years and is still owned by the original Dunham family. Nearby Bash-Bish Falls is considered the most spectacular in Massachusetts. Great Barrington is believed to have the only street anywhere to be named for a counterfeiter — Belcher Square. The house in Great Barrington where William Cullen Bryant lived for many years may still be seen. A more unusual house is the weird Gingerbread House of Tyringham. It has to be seen to be believed. Henry H. Kitson, sculptor of Lexington's Minuteman, built the house as a studio. Two tons (about 1.8 metric tons) of nails went into the rolling roof, which has a built-in witch's face. Since 1953 it has been used as a gallery for contemporary art.

Nathaniel Hawthorne made Tanglewood and the Berkshires famous through his *Tanglewood Tales*. The cottage where he wrote one of his best-known works, *The House of the Seven Gables,* may be seen in replica. Today the name of Tanglewood is known for the Berkshire Music Festival held there each year in a beautiful 210 acre (about 85 hectares) wooded setting, amid formal and informal gardens with mountain vistas. The Music Shed seats 6,000 music lovers who hear the Boston Symphony and other attractions without amplification, due to extraordinary acoustics of the Memorial Stage Canopy. Classes in music for advanced students are also held.

For 267 years the historic Old Elm grew in City Hall Park at Pittsfield. At one time Lucretia Williams placed herself between the tree and woodmen who were assigned to chop it down, and saved the venerable tree with her own body. However, later it was struck by lightning, and had to be cut down.

Pittsfield, with its beautiful mountain setting, is a cultural center, supporting a Temple of Music, the Berkshire Museum of Natural History and Art, and the Athenaeum, especially known for its collection of materials on Herman Melville. The first agricultural fair in America was held at Pittsfield in 1810.

At Dalton, the museum of the Crane Paper Company is one of the finest of its type. The firm has been making fine papers since the Revolution, and the museum especially features its currency papers.

The 30-foot (about 9 meters) span of the natural bridge near North Adams makes it the largest marble formation of its type. The autumn colors which glorify so much of Massachusetts are especially recognized at the Fall Foliage Festival in North Adams. The 90-foot (about 27 meters) Greylock War Memorial to Massachusetts' veterans was built in 1932 at a cost of $200,000. It crowns the summit of Massachusetts' highest point, Mt. Greylock. Thunderbolt Ski Run of Mt. Greylock plunges right into the town of Adams.

Williams College in Williamstown remembers an unusual event in an unusual way—with its unique Haystack Monument. The story is

Williamstown.

told that a group of devout Williams College students met in an out-of-the-way place to pray for the beginning of missionary work in far lands. When it began to rain, they took shelter under a haystack. The Student Volunteer Movement *did* lead to the sending of American missionaries to all continents, and the monument commemorates this historic beginning.

In fact, wherever the visitor goes in Massachusetts he realizes that he is living an experience of the past in a land of historic beginnings, where history and progress continue to go hand in hand.

Handy Reference Section

Instant Facts
Official name—Commonwealth of Massachusetts
Became the sixth state, February 6, 1788
Capital—Boston, founded 1630
Nickname—The Bay State
State motto—*Ense petit placidam sub liberate quietem* (By the sword we seek peace,
               but peace only under liberty)
State animal—Morgan horse
State bird—Chickadee *(Penthestes atricapillies)*
State fish—Cod *(Gadus morrhua)*
State tree—American elm *(Ulmus Americana)*
State flower—Mayflower *(Epigaea repens,* also known as trailing arbutus or ground
               laurel)
State song—"All Hail to Massachusetts," words and music by Arthur J. Marsh
Area—8,093 square miles (20,961 square kilometers)
Rank in area—45th
Coastline—192 miles (309 kilometers)
Shoreline—1,519 miles (2,445 kilometers)
Greatest length, north to south—110 miles (177 kilometers)
Greatest width, east to west—190 miles (306 kilometers)
Geographic center—North part of the city of Worcester
Highest point—3,491 feet (1,064 meters), Mt. Greylock
Lowest point—Sea level
Number of counties—14
Population—6,277,000 (1980 projection)
Rank in population—10th
Population density—775.6 per square mile (299.5 per square kilometer), based on
               1980 projection
Rank in density—3rd
Population center—In Natick town, Middlesex County, 15.5 miles (24.9
               kilometers) southwest of Cambridge
Birthrate—12.4 per 1,000
Physicians per 100,000—222
Principal cities—Boston

Boston	637,986 (1975 state census)
Worcester	172,342
Springfield	168,785
Cambridge	102,095
New Bedford	100,345
Fall River	100,339
Brockton	95,688
Quincy	91,487

You Have a Date with History

1497-1498—John Cabot touches Massachusetts
1524—Giovanni de Verrazano passes coast
1606—Samuel de Champlain visits Stage Harbor
1620—Pilgrims reach the New World, Plymouth founded
1622—Weymouth founded
1630—Puritans settle Boston area
1636—Beginnings of Harvard
1675—Settlers battle King Philip
1691—Massachusetts becomes a Royal Colony
1704—First newspaper published in America appears at Boston
1763—Massachusetts suffers in French and Indian War
1773—Boston Tea Party
1775—Revolution!
1776—Enemy troops leave Massachusetts
1780—Massachusetts constitution approved
1788—Statehood
1796—Massachusetts' John Adams elected President
1820—First of more liberal reforms
1824—Massachusetts' John Quincy Adams elected President
1832—Antislavery Society formed in Boston
1846—Anesthetics used successfully first in Boston
1867—Mary Baker Eddy begins Christian Science teaching
1914—Cape Cod Canal opened
1919—Boston police strike
1923—Massachusetts' Calvin Coolidge becomes President
1936—Harvard three hundred years old
1957—*Mayflower II* arrives
1961—Massachusetts' John F. Kennedy becomes President
1963—President Kennedy assassinated
1965—Centennary of Massachusetts' anti-discrimination law
1971—State government reorganized
1978—Massive winter storms, parts of the state declared disaster areas

Thinkers, Doers, Fighters

People of renown who have been associated with Massachusetts

Adams, John
Adams, John Quincy
*Adams, Samuel
Alger, Horatio
Anthony, Susan B.
Attucks, Crispus
Baldwin, Loammi
Bell, Alexander Graham
Bigelow, Erastus
Billings, William
Bradford, William
Bryant, William Cullen
Bulfinch, Charles
Bull, Ephraim
Butterick, Ebenezer
Channing, William Ellery
Coolidge, Calvin
Cotton, John
Dennison, Aaron
Dickinson, Emily
Dix, Dorothea L.
Eddy, Mary Baker
Edwards, Jonathan
Eliot, T.S.
Emerson, Ralph Waldo
Everett, Edward
Field, Eugene
Franklin, Benjamin
French, Daniel Chester
Frost, Robert
Gardner, Mrs. John Lowell
Garrison, William Lloyd
Hancock, John
Harvard, John
Hawthorne, Nathaniel

Hawes, Russell
Holmes, Oliver Wendell
Homer, Winslow
Howe, Julia Ward
James, William
Kennedy, John Fitzgerald
Lodge, Henry Cabot
Longfellow, Henry Wadsworth
Lowell, Amy
Lowell, John and John Jr.
Lowell, Francis Cabot
MacMillan, Donald B.
Mann, Horace
Massasoit (Chief)
Moody, Dwight Lyman
Morse, Samuel F.B.
Morton, William T.G.
O'Neill, Eugene
Palmer, Alice Freeman
Peabody, George
Philip (King)
Poe, Edgar Allan
Post, Emily
Radcliffe, Ann
Revere, Paul
Smith, Samuel
Smith, Sophia
Standish, Miles
Thoreau, Henry David
Van Rensselaer, Stephen
Ward, Artemus
Whistler, James Abbott McNeill
Whittier, John Greenleaf
Winthrop, John

*Massachusetts' representative in Statuary Hall of the Capital, Washington, D.C.

Governors of the Commonwealth of Massachusetts

John Hancock 1780-1785
James Bowdoin 1785-1787
John Hancock 1787-1793
Samuel Adams 1793-1797
Increase Sumner 1797-1799
Moses Gill 1799-1800
Caleb Strong 1800-1807
James Sullivan 1807-1808
Levi Lincoln 1808-1809
Christopher Gore 1809-1810
Elbridge Gerry 1810-1812
Caleb Strong 1812-1816
John Brooks 1816-1823
William Eustis 1823-1825
Marcus Morton 1825
Levi Lincoln, Jr. 1825-1834
John Davis 1834-1835
Samuel T. Armstrong 1835-1836
Edward Everett 1836-1840
Marcus Morton 1840-1841
John Davis 1841-1843
Marcus Morton 1843-1844
George N. Briggs 1844-1851
George S. Boutwell 1851-1853
John H. Clifford 1853-1854
Emory Washburn 1854-1855
Henry J. Gardner 1855-1858
Nathaniel P. Banks 1858-1861
John A. Andrew 1861-1866
Alex H. Bullock 1866-1869
William Claflin 1869-1872
William B. Washburn 1872-1874
Thomas Talbot 1874-1875
William Gaston 1875-1876
Alex H. Rice 1876-1879

Thomas Talbot 1879-1880
John D. Long 1880-1883
Benjamin F. Butler 1883-1884
George D. Robinson 1884-1887
Oliver Ames 1887-1890
John Q.A. Brackett 1890-1891
William E. Russell 1891-1894
Frederick T. Greenhaige 1894-1896
Roger Wolcott 1896-1900
W. Murray Crane 1900-1903
John L. Bates 1903-1905
William L. Douglas 1905-1906
Curtis Guild, Jr. 1906-1909
Eben S. Draper 1909-1911
Eugene N. Foss 1911-1914
David I. Walsh 1914-1916
Samuel W. McCall 1916-1918
Calvin Coolidge 1919-1921
Channing H. Cox 1921-1925
Alvan T. Fuller 1925-1929
Frank G. Allen 1929-1931
Joseph B. Ely 1931-1935
James M. Curley 1935-1937
Charles F. Hurley 1937-1939
Leverett Saltonstall 1939-1945
Maurice J. Tobin 1945-1947
Robert F. Bradford 1947-1949
Paul A. Dever 1949-1953
Christian A. Herter 1953-1957
Foster Furcolo 1957-1961
John A. Volpe 1961-1963
Endicott Peabody 1963-1965
John A. Volpe 1965-1969
Francis W. Sargent 1969-1975
Michael Dukakis 1975-

Index

95

PICTURE CREDITS

Color photographs courtesy of the following: Division of Tourism, Massachusetts Department of Commerce and Development, pages 11, 16, 21, 32 (bottom), 43, 44, 46, 47, 51, 57, 70, and 81; American Airlines, pages 8, 58, 78, and 84; Department of the Army, Corps of Engineers, New England Division, page 12; Allan Carpenter, page 23; The Witch House, Salem, page 26; Travelers Insurance Company, page 30; Old North Church, Boston, page 32 (top); USDA, Robert Hailstock, Jr., page 55; Massachusetts Historical Society, page 60; United Air Lines, Inc., pages 65 and 74, TWA, page 72.

Illustrations on pages 35, 48, 68, and back cover by Len W. Meents.

ABOUT THE AUTHOR

With the publication of his first book for school use when he was twenty, **Allan Carpenter** began a career as an author that has spanned more than 135 books. After teaching in the public schools of Des Moines, Mr. Carpenter began his career as an educational publisher at the age of twenty-one when he founded the magazine *Teachers Digest.* In the field of educational periodicals, he was responsible for many innovations. During his many years in publishing, he has perfected a highly organized approach to handling large volumes of factual material: after extensive traveling and having collected all possible materials, he systematically reviews and organizes everything. From his apartment high in Chicago's John Hancock Building, Allan recalls, "My collection and assimilation of materials on the states and countries began before the publication of my first book." Allan is the founder of Carpenter Publishing House and of Infordata International, Inc., publishers of *Issues in Education* and *Index to U. S. Government Periodicals.* When he is not writing or traveling, his principal avocation is music. He has been the principal bassist of many symphonies, and he managed the country's leading non-professional symphony for twenty-five years.